GOSPELS
OPENED

AMBASSADOR
Belfast • Greenville

THE
GOSPELS
OPENED

by

J. Stuart Holden, M.A.

The Gospels Opened

ISBN 1 898787 40 9

Published by

AMBASSADOR PRODUCTIONS, LTD.
Providence House
16 Hillview Avenue,
Belfast, BT5 6JR

Emerald House
1 Chick Springs Road, Suite 102
Greenville, South Carolina, 29609

FOREWORD

The purpose of this volume is to afford help in the daily gathering of the Manna to those who come to the Holy Word for spiritual sustenance and strength. It is not in any sense designed as a Commentary, nor yet as an aid to Bible Study (of which there are so many available), but rather as an encouragement to devotional reading. It aims at being of use to the large numbers of Christians who, with little time for regular study, are keenly desirous of getting something from the morning or evening chapter to help nourish their souls, being conscious that it is only by feeding thus on God's Word that His people are built up in holy character and stengthened for the serious business of Christian service. Anything like a full exposition of the sacred text is not even attempted. In each chapter one prominent thought is selected for meditation, and some simple suggestions offered as to its meaning and practical application to personal life. At best, these are but crumbs from the Loaf, gleams from the Sun, tiny grains of gold-dust from the Mine, whose great value is in their testimony to the supreme worth of the Whole.

Nothing is more needed in our common life today than recovery by the ordinary Christian of the spiritual values of the Word of God. It is at once our Chart, our Lamp, our Food, our Sword. And in all these ways it may be known by the humblest believer who yields himself to the illumination of the Divine Spirit - its Author. It was not given originally in order to make men scholars, but rather that they should by its means become sons and saints, servants and soldiers of the Most High. It is the glory of the Bible that while its heights and depths are so great that no human learning can scale or sound them unaided, its Treasure-house is yet unlocked to the simplest believer by the golden key of obedience. As a Book it differs from every other book in this respect, that it demands the setting up of a sympathetic relationship before it yields its riches to the reader. Until a man is honestly seeking to walk in the truth it has already proclaimed to him, he can receive nothing further. Failure of obedience invests its every message with a tone of utter condemnation. For it reveals on its every page the Christ Who is set for the rise or fall of every soul that comes into contact with Him, so they determine what shall be the unchanging personal message of the Book. And so do they come either to love or to loathe it. Right well has it been said that 'this Book will keep you from sin, or sin will keep you from this Book'. For of both Old and New Testaments alike it is true, that 'these are they which testify of ME.'

In these days there are not wanting all around us those whose subtle attacks upon the Divine inspiration of the Word, and its conse-quent unique authority in all matters of faith and practice, are hard to repel by the average Christian. While very certain that scholarship must and can be met by scholarship, and that the Book is no sort of danger from its critics, it is obvious also that this course is only available to a few at most. The largest numbers of Christians have to be content to look on at the struggle, sometimes perplexed as to its progress, and often confused as to its issues. But each one of us may at the same time have a personal and ever-increasing sense of the Divinity of the Bible, which is entirely unaffected by the pros and cons of any merely aca-demic contest. The facts that in its pages God daily speaks to our hearts, that it finds us at the deepest levels of our need, that its precepts being obeyed, its promises are also realised, and that in it we meet the Lord Christ Himself - a Living, Bright Reality, cannot be explained away by any speciousness of hypothesis or conclusion of argument. The ulti-mate proof is the subjective one, of which every man who daily feeds upon God's Word becomes increasingly aware. The experience of all such is an irrefutable testimony that this is the very Word of the Lord. And it is to the creation and enlargement of such experience that it is hoped these notes may contribute.

No man, however, who treats the Holy Word with anything less than the utmost reverence and deference can hope to realise these things. There are many amongst those who are bidden who do not taste of the Royal Feast. And the fault is always their own. Hasty, casual, irregular readers do despite to the Scriptures, and have to bear the consequences in their own lives. For it is only the Word hidden carefully in the heart that ensures victory in the sharp and sudden conflict with temptation. It is only the Word diligently heeded that cleanses the ways of life. It is only as we sit down unhurriedly under His Shadow with great delight that His Fruit becomes sweet to our taste, stimulating and strengthening us for toil. Failure in these respects is entire failure.

Let us then cultivate regular and conscience-bound habits with regard to the daily trust with our Lord. As He was found in the Garden, the Divine Conqueror of sin and death, by those whose instincts of love took them thither in the early morning, so He is daily to be met in the narrow highways and spacious pastures of the Word, by those who make it their earliest and chief concern to have speech with Him. And if eyes and ears should not be quick to recognise Him, do not hurry away. Rather wait still upon God with the prayer -

Open my eyes that I may see
Glimpses of truth Thou hast for me,
Place in my hands the wonderful key
That shall unclasp, and set me free.
Silently now I wait for Thee,
Ready, my God, Thy Will to see;
Open my eyes, illumine me,
Spirit Divine!

Open my ears, that I may hear
Voices of truth Thou sendest clear;
And while the wave-notes fall on my ear,
Everything false will disappear.
Silently now I wait for Thee,
Ready, my God, Thy Will to see;
Open my ears, illumine me,
Spirit Divine!

Nor can there be any disappointment. None that wait for Him shall be ashamed. For He ever fulfils the desire of them that fear Him, with such completeness, that new-clad in the Heaven-forged armour, and with renewed inspiration and quickened purpose, they go forth to the walk and warfare of life to be more than conquerors. There is no other way of life than by this Word of the Lord.

J. Stuart Holden

St. MATTHEW

CHAPTER I

" Thou shalt call His name Jesus, for He shall save His people from their sins" (v. 21).

IN these words the New Testament declares on its first page the whole subject of its contents. All that is subsequently found within the various Books which go to make up the whole is but an expansion and an unfolding of this great Evangel. It is alike the theme of the angelic announcement at the beginning of the volume, and of the triumphant exultation of the redeemed at the end. Nor is there any intervening page of the sacred Scriptures which is not superscribed with the Saviour's own words: "These are they which testify of Me." With what reverence and humility, then, should we approach a Book with a message of such personal significance and eternal import to each one of us! Here, if anywhere, are the issues of life and death.

Such a word as this is all-comprehensive of the Saviour's purpose and power. While primarily it foretells the unspeakable and mysterious transaction in which He made atonement for the sin of the world, by taking upon Himself the weight of its guilt, and offering Himself a redemptive sacrifice, this by no means exhausts its significance. For though that great fact is both basal and central of all true life, the starting-point of all vital faith and the beginning of all living hope, its application to individual heart and life is all-important and is equally indicated.

" He shall save His people from their sins " ! Not merely from their penalty, by His death; but from their power, by His life. Every devastating result of sin He purposes to repair. Every deteriorated capacity He covenants to recreate. Every enslavement of memory and power He can break. Every usurping ruler of the heart He will drive out. And every antagonism of holiness which is part of the entail of sin He is able to transform and convert into loyalty. What a tremendous claim is this ! And what a wealth of experience in every age attests its justification ! Let us put His Saviourhood to the practical test of our own salvation, not from any unseen and future terror, but from every realized and present thraldom. In this way only can we *know* Him whom to know is life eternal.

CHAPTER II

"Where is He that is born King?" (*v.* 2).

MATTHEW is essentially the evangelist of
Christ's Kingship. In the pages of his Gospel
we see Him moving amongst men with a sup-
porting consciousness of authority, manifested
as the Divine Sovereign whose Kingdom is not
of this world. The coming of the Wise Men
from the East to worship at His rude cradle
is strikingly prophetic of that homage which
shall one day be given to Him, when in His
Name every knee shall bow. If His infant
days are beclouded by the foreshadowing of
the Cross, they are also brightened by the foreglow of the Kingdom.

"Where is He that is born King?" is a
question which we may profitably put to ourselves. For, too often alas, even by those who
profess to believe and serve Him, He is denied
the throne. Men are not unwilling to accept
His grace, if that can be done without yielding
to His government. They are glad to have
Him near to the precincts of life, in case they
should come to need Him; but they will not
allow Him its presidency, in case He should
come to *need them!* Indeed, the common cause
of the powerlessness and ineffectiveness of so

much avowed Christian life to-day is to be
sought in the failure to recognize Christ as King,
and to realize His unquestioned control. For
when "His Kingdom ruleth over all," life is
invested with the sanctifying power which increasingly delivers it from all that is sordid and
unworthy in motive and aim ; and at the same
time inspires to self-forgetting service. But
when He is not so enthroned, life's course runs
on to increasing weakness and worthlessness,
and its true end is lost. The gold, frankincense,
and myrrh, lovingly bestowed upon Him, are
strangely multiplied to the enrichment of the
worshipper, as well as to the service of the
Saviour. But, selfishly withheld from Him,
they become a positive impoverishment. His
enthronement conditions our moral and spiritual
enduement ; and hence, no consideration can
be quite so important as this present one—
." *Where* is He that is born King ? "

CHAPTER III

"*Fruits meet for repentance*" (*v.* 8).

CHRIST's herald leaves no room for doubt as
to the character of Him whom He proclaims,
nor as to the nature of the claims He makes
upon those to whom He comes as Saviour and
Sovereign. The message of John the Baptist

is, in this respect, both a preparation and a
prophecy, to which we, along with those who
first heard it, do well to take earnest heed.
Its penetrating declaration is that faith is a
force making for entire righteousness of life,
and that sincere repentance is to be attested
by scrupulous obedience to apprehended light.
Approach to God is not to be made along a
road of mere mental and emotional activity,
but by the painful way of self-amendment. If
men are to compass His altar, their hands
must be washed in innocency. Fruitless repentance is faithless.

Is this word not needed to-day? Is there
no danger of our becoming content with mere
mental apprehensions of truth and duty, without
personal concern for matters of practical conduct? Do we not often contradict our sacred
profession by continued indulgence in things
doubtful, or even openly sinful? Is not this
the charge brought, too often with justification,
against Christians by the unbelieving world?
And does this fact not emphasize our individual
responsibility to lay this word to heart?

But while such fruit as is " meet for repentance " demands on our part honest labour for
its cultivation, we must bear in mind that
all such moral effort is in co-operation with the
Divine forces of righteousness. Just as in
Nature the farmer labours at the soil, but it is

the sun and shower and wind which make his
work effective, so in the field of life and character.
True repentance is the fruit of the Spirit. And
yet the command to us is to " bring forth ! "

CHAPTER IV

" It is written " (*vv.* 4, 7, 10).

WHETHER in Christ or His followers, the
Adversary challenges every spiritual position
which faith assumes. The opening Heaven
has scarcely closed, the descending Dove has
hardly settled, the approving Voice has only
just ceased, when the Saviour is in grips with
the foe. His conflict and conquest at the very
commencement of life are a forecast of all that
awaits Him in the pathway of obedience to the
Father's will; for toward the close of His life
He summarizes the whole experience of His
earthly days which His disciples have shared
with Him, as " My temptations." Thus it was
that He partook of the common lot of every man,
being " tempted in all points like as we are."
And His example in repelling the enemy is for
ever our guide into the life of victory.

Note His ready use of the sacred Scriptures,
evidencing a familiarity with them which was
only gained by diligent study and a careful
hiding of them in His heart as the very words

of God, during the silent and unrecorded years
at Nazareth. Knowledge of the Divine precept, and promise, and power, is the first
prerequisite for successful. emergence in
any encounter. Neglect of the Word may be
secret and hidden from all eyes, but will surely
manifest itself in the crises of temptation which
find us unprepared. " Moreover by them is
Thy servant warned," and to be forewarned is
to be forearmed indeed. Let us assure ourselves
of victory, therefore, in our silent hours of
fellowship.

Note also that each of the Saviour's answers
is a re-assertion of the very position which the
enemy assails. " If Thou be the Son of God "
is the challenge, to which faith responds by
declaring a determination of those principles of
conduct which are vital to sonship, i. e. depen-
dence, loyalty, and obedience. Against these
no temptation can succeed ; for to the man who
fearlessly asserts them, despite his consciousness of personal weakness, comes a reinforce-
ment of Divine power which carries him through.
And, like the Saviour, such an one is ministered
to by the angels of God in his hour of reaction,
and when the glow of the conflict has died
down. God Himself is at his right hand, and he
shall not be moved.

CHAPTER V

"Ye are the light of the world" (*v.* 14).

BEHIND this declaration is an implied miracle. Christ's followers can only shine as lights in the world's gloom when all the darkness of their own hearts has been expelled by His Divine power. Indeed, the whole of their qualifying experience is on this wise; for with them, as with Him, it is the *life* which is the light of men. No mere mental apprehension of truth is adequate, except in so far as it leads to the transformation of character by submission and obedience to its power. For mark well the nature of the light with which, as Christians, we are to illumine the surrounding darkness. As the spectroscope of the scientist reveals the various primary colours of which the white ray of sunlight is composed, so the words of the Master immediately precedent to these, give us to understand what are the components of that reflective holiness which makes us " children of the light." Poverty of spirit—that is, absence of pride and self-sufficiency; sincerity of repentance which mourns over past sin; meekness of disposition; earnest desire after righteousness; merciful kindness toward others; entire purity of heart and purpose—all go to make up that

type of life which Christ here describes. And all
emphasize the necessity of the miracle. For
these are qualities which none can acquire,
except by the redeeming energy of the Son of
God Himself.

It is noteworthy that Christ assumes this
when He says: "Let your light shine." In
other words, He implies that the imparted
Divine nature, which is the outcome of our
union with Him, will certainly declare itself,
unless it be hindered. He suggests, also, the
commonest hindrance of all, under the figure
of the bushel. For it is absorption of heart in the
cares and commerce of life thus represented
which dims the light of many an one, and
ultimately extinguishes it altogether. The
"bushel" is a necessity in every life; but why
not invert and turn it into a lamp-stand?
Why not regard every imperative contact with
the world of business and social life as a God-
planned opportunity of illuminating the darkness which is immediately around us? For so
indeed it is. Only so will the facts of our
lives correspond with this declaration of Christ;
and only so will men, seeing us, glorify our
Heavenly Father, whose light of love and
power we thus radiate.

CHAPTER VI

" *Our Father* " (*v.* 9).

THE whole purpose of Christ's coming may be
defined as the revelation of God as the Father.
Prior to His day, even the best and most enlightened conception of Him fell far short of this ;
and in consequence there was lacking from the
life of those who most truly sought Him that
relationship of filial love and obedience which is
the whole of true religion. At the foundation of
Christ's Gospel lies the eternal fact of the father-
liness of God ; and the import of His own life
amongst men is the unfolding of this, the Divine
character. His works of mercy and power are
the Father's. His words of grace and life are the
Father's. The will, which is the inspiring cause
of all His travail and toil, is the Father's. And
in the end, His suffering and sacrifice is just the
Father's love in its contact with human sin.

The key-note of His Evangel is that men
become sons of the Father, not by natural
generation but by spiritual regeneration ; not
by their first birth but by a second and new
birth, which is effected as they receive Him into
heart and life, in faith and obedience. Then to
all such He teaches this lesson of prayer : " After
this manner . . . Our Father."

Note the plural form enjoined. Relationship with the Father brings us into relationship with the family also. The Fatherhood of God revealed in the Saviourhood of Christ is the basis of true brotherhood. It is "with *all* the saints" that we come to know the extent of His love and power. And it is therefore with them all that we pray.

And further He is "the God and Father of our Lord Jesus Christ," who teaches us thus to unite ourselves with Him as we pray. What an encouragement is this to those who are cast down, and almost afraid to approach God, because of conscious shortcoming and unworthiness! We do not come to Him alone, but along with the Saviour-Advocate, who bids us call Him "Our Father"—His and ours.

CHAPTER VII

"*How much more shall your Father which is in Heaven give good things to them that ask Him*" (*v.* 11).

ALL human excellence of character is at best but a feeble reflection of the Divine. The love and foresight of an earthly father, which secures as far as may be the highest good of his child, is only a remote echo of the affection and wisdom of God. To be assured of this is the secret of perfect peace, and the inspiration of all confident prayer. In our asking, seeking, and knocking—which represent degrees of increasing importunity in supplication—we have the unfailing encouragement of the goodwill of our Father. Hence, however urgent our prayer, it is never to be regarded as an overcoming of His reluctance, but rather as a laying-hold of His covenanted willingness to bless. We have no need to " storm the gate of Heaven " by our beseeching. For He waits to be gracious to us at all times.

Note the limitation which Christ here expresses. He does not promise that we shall receive all that we ask ; for often we ask amiss. The greatest calamity that could befall us would be to have some of our prayers literally answered, and some of our desires actually fulfilled. And just here we see most clearly the wonderful conjunction of the Father's love and wisdom. An earthly parent may love his child foolishly to his hurt, indulging his every wish to his undoing. But our Heavenly Father gives only " good things "—things that are for our highest wellbeing, things that will minister to our surest development in holiness of life and character. This is the explanation of the many seemingly unanswered petitions which have sometimes disturbed our faith in prayer. God may deny, but He never despises any of our petitions. His " No " is just as truly an answer as His " Yes " could have been. The things He withholds are only those that are not good for us. He never fails to supply our need, nor to correct our notions. And no *good* thing is ever withheld from him who walks uprightly.

Remember that this was even so with the Saviour Himself. His prayer for the removal of the last bitter cup was not granted. But in its stead an angel ministry was given ! We are wise children when we leave the choice of our " good things " to our Father.

CHAPTER VIII

" There arose a great tempest . . . Then He arose " (*v.* 24–6).

THE greatest difficulty in many a life comes with the storm which arises after Christ has been accepted, and when the honest following of Him has begun. When men commence loyally to carry out His instructions, a tempest of opposition often seems to break furiously upon them ; and danger to the little craft of life seems imminent. Now, it is well to remember that the greatest havoc any storm can cause is not in the loss of material things, not in the wreck of the boat and its gear, but in the weakening and destruction of faith. To conclude that God is somehow indifferent, is at once to expose the

feebleness of our trust and our tragic ignorance
of Him. For when we seem to be overwhelmed,
we are really overshadowed. When we imagine
we are being deserted, we are only being dis-
ciplined. When the storm-clouds lower and the
waves threaten to engulf us, we need to remind
ourselves that " He maketh the clouds His
chariots, and walketh upon the wings of the
wind ; " and to look out for Him in and through
these very things.

For He is never far away from us in the hour
of our danger ; and above the howling of the
tempest He can hear the feeblest cry for help.
And what more sufficient help can we have than
just to be assured of His presence ? The blackest
darkness which ever enwraps the soul is not that
of sorrow, or trial, or loss ; but of inability to
realize His nearness. For did He but forsake us,
all would indeed be lost. But how safe are those
who can stay their souls upon His promise to be
with them even when they pass through the
waters ! And what wondering love fills their
hearts who experience the great calm of spirit
which His presence creates !

CHAPTER IX

" *Follow Me* " (*v*. 9).

THIS is the whole call of the Gospel comprehended in a word which is at once an invitation and a demand. It indicates the way out of every sin-maze, and the path through every tangled territory of duty or difficulty. It cuts the Gordian knot of every moral and spiritual perplexity, and points the bewildered soul with saving clearness to the road of life. To accept and obey it, is to realize an established fellowship with the Saviour which is a partnership of power. To decline its call, is to miss all that makes for true joy, and to lose every essential of the life that is life indeed.

The history of Matthew the publican to whom Christ addressed this call, and his subsequent experience upon responding to it, is full of instruction and encouragement to us. To begin with, he was a man who had failed and forfeited all claim to consideration. As a Levite, he had already been privileged to engage in the service of God, which for some reason he had deserted ; and Christ's call came as a renewed opportunity —a second chance. How great is the love which reaches down lower than our failure and self-despair, in order to lift us up ! When we have been overcome by the seductive charms of the world, and entangled in its snares, so that we forsake Him entirely, He is still near us, and does not for one moment forget us. It is of His unchanging grace that He never gives us up.

And with the call to arise and leave all that has ensnared and held—the golden bonds of the world's forging—comes the imparted power of obedience. Christ's word is instinct with dynamic, so that the man who resolutely sets himself to make the determining choice finds himself miraculously strengthened to take the directed step. And every successive step depends entirely on the taking of this initial one. Christ is first recognized, then trusted, and then followed; and along that pathway of discipleship there lies for Matthew and for us unspeakable blessing. It inevitably leads to a varied experience in which light and darkness closely impinge, in which joy is often neighboured by suffering, and in which the love of God is strangely mingled with the reproach of men. Indeed, since it is a following of Him to which we are committed, it must lead us round by the Cross, and make us partakers of its pain. But it leads us on to share His risen life in all its redemptive influences; and thus to realize our own highest possibilities in soul-winning service.

Are we prepared thus to follow Him? For He calls us to-day as ever.

CHAPTER X

" I came not to send peace, but a sword" (v. 34).

At first sight it almost seems as if this self-declaration of Christ is in direct contradiction of all that we have been led to look for in the Prince of Peace. For He plainly declares that His mission is that of the sword. That there is no inconsistency, however, in this, we are assured when we remember that first and last He came to save men from sin. Where sin is found, there can be no peace except such as follows the sword. In the deepest sense of all, He must fail of His redeeming purpose if He comes into the field of human need not having His sword girt upon His thigh.

Of course His speech is figurative, illustrating for all time the certain effect, both in individual life and in society generally, of true and saving apprehension of Him. The first dawning of Christ-consciousness inevitably strikes a deadly blow at sin, destroying vain desires, unholy imaginings, and base loves; bringing the smart of sorrow, regret, and remorse into life. As that consciousness of Him increases, and we come to know Him better, it is as though successive blows were aimed at our self-complacency and satisfaction. For His ideals of life are always sword-edged;

and the enlightened heart inevitably becomes
a battle-field. Further still, as we embrace the
privilege and duty of witnessing to Him in the
world, we realize that He is the Christ of the
sword. For we find immediately that His very
command to make our faith visible is a cut at
our hindering relationships. Who does not know
the severance between friend and friend—even
between child and parent, husband and wife—
which the sword of Christ makes? Do not let
us shrink from Him, however, on this account.
For the forging of His sword was in the fires of
Gethsemane and Calvary, and the Hand that
wields it for our blessing is nail-pierced.

Then, too, in the world generally, Christ is
eternally at war with all that is wrong—with
selfishness, injustice, and oppression. He is
manifested to destroy the works of the devil;
and this He does through His people. They
become in His hand as a sword against all that
is opposed to the will of God. It is through
their yielded lives that all His redeeming energy
is brought to bear upon the sin-created com-
plexities which are on every hand; and it is by
them that He conquers fresh territory and sets
up His Kingdom in men's hearts. Let us then
not shun the conflict, for its issue is never in
doubt; and it is only through the strife that we
shall at last come to sing the song of the victor.

CHAPTER XI

" Come . . . take . . . learn " (*vv.* 28–9).

So simple are Christ's words in this prescrip-
tion for rest of soul, that a little child can understand them at once. But it often takes grown
men a long time to become as little children, in
practical obedience to a demand which is an
invitation, and to an invitation which is a
demand. For we are prone to stagger at " the
simplicity that is in Christ "; and love's stepping-
stones across the turbulent waters of unrest into
the green pastures of peace become stones of
stumbling to us.

" *Come !* " Christ gently suggests that we
have been living too far away from Him. It
may be that our deeds have been evil ; and so
we have feared to come to the light. Or, the
lawful occupations of life, its duties and delights,
its tools and toys, have become a positive engrossment to us. Or, we have absorbed ourselves in our personal concerns of joy or sorrow.
But whatever be the cause, we are living too far
away from Christ ; and to come to Him involves
our coming away from every engrossment, and
our renunciation of all that cannot be brought
into His presence. This is the first step upon
which all else depends.

" *Take !* " Life's central government must be

changed, if the old unrest is not to creep back
into the forgiven heart, and if we are to " find
rest " in the labours and burdens of which life
is full. The Saviour must become the Sovereign.
The kingdom must pass under His control.
Christ's will must dethrone self-will, and His
purpose must become the passion of our lives.
Then, just as the ordinary wooden yoke of
agricultural use unites the strength of oxen for
the work of a common task, so the yoke of
Christ assures a conference of power to the
yielded soul. It means that the one who accepts
His authority no longer lives a single life with
all its limitations and disabilities, but a life of
union with Him in whom all power is vested.
To take Christ's yoke is just to accept His
commission to daily duty in the certainty of His
abundant enduement for the task.

" *Learn !* " Of this we cannot fail, if the
earlier steps are honestly taken. As men company with Christ, they come instinctively to refer
everything to His judgement and to test everything by His standards. This is, of course,
a state rather than a step. For there is so much
to unlearn and to undo, to lose and to acquire,
that life itself is not long enough for the whole
lesson. But to the one who is willing to learn,
Christ will both unlock heavenly treasures and
explain earthly mysteries, in such a way as to
bring increasing rest and peace to the world-

wearied and self-tired heart. And there is no other way of peace than these three words indicate.

CHAPTER XII

" *He that is not with Me is against Me* " (*v.* 30).

THERE is something startling in words which seem to invest Christ with a quality akin to narrowness and intolerance. We are accustomed to think of Him as being so full of love as to be without asperities of any kind ; and as of such broad tolerance and appreciation as to make this claim appear in entire contrast with His character. And yet on quiet thought we find that this statement is not contradictory but complementary. For if He is intolerant it is not with the intolerance of earth, which is usually the expression of fragmentary and imperfect knowledge, but with that of Heaven—the expression of entire insight and understanding. He knows, for instance, the subtlety and strength of the sin from which He has come to save men ; and the full value also of those capacities and aptitudes which He seeks to deliver from the grip of the destructive forces which rob God of His rights. With such knowledge, He would be less Divine than He is, were

He not intolerant of every rival. The issues
involved are so vital that He would be less our
Saviour than He is, did He not declare them so
plainly.

Note how this high strain characterizes all His
teaching. We find it in the nature of His self-
claims : " I am *the* Light of the world ; " " I am
the Bread of life ; " " I am *the* Way, *the* Truth,
and *the* Life." Again we see it in the commands
which He lays upon His followers : " Seek ye
first the Kingdom of God ; " " Follow thou *Me*."
And yet again is it expressed in His imposition
of self-discipline upon the honest disciple : " If
thine eye offend thee, pluck it out. If thine
hand offend thee, cut it off ! " In all this we
see God in contact with human life, and recognize Divine intolerance in the word which challenges every other lord, which summons us from
every other absorption, and which forbids any
disloyal and disastrous tolerance of sin. Only as
invested with this character could it be the Word
of Life to us.

But it is in respect of His discrimination of
men that Christ is most unmistakable and
definite. In moral issues, mere neutrality is
quite impossible ; and it is of the nature of love
to make this indubitably clear. We are compelled to take sides when brought into the circle
of His influence ; and He declares that it is our
spiritual sympathies which pronounce upon us.

The one who is not *with* Him in all the active sympathics of life, who is not living in obedient agreement with His programme, who is not working in loyal co-operation with His power—based upon personal faith in Himself—is *against* Him.

How much do we need this reminder in an age of specious but spurious toleration of everything which is professedly " religious " ! The broad-mindedness of our day finds no justification in Christ. In so far as we really know Him, we cannot be tolerant of anything that derogates from His glory as Saviour and Redeemer. And though our intolerance must be free from all bitterness, it cannot be less marked than His own. Nor can we company with those who assign Him any place lower than the highest of all.

CHAPTER XIII

" *Treasure hid in a field* " (*v.* 44).

THIS is one of the most vivid of Christ's Parables of the Kingdom of Heaven. It is the story of a ploughman, who, following the plough, finds the course of his furrow impeded by some heavy object, which on examination proves to be an iron box in which is a hidden hoard of gold. On an instant his prospects are changed from poverty to affluence; and in order to realize them, he sells all that he possesses, and becomes the owner both of field and treasure.

Its possible interpretation is twofold, at the same time illustrating the Divine and emphasizing the human side also of the great transaction by which men become partakers of the Kingdom. For the treasure hid in a field points to the worth of the individual soul, which though it may be unrecognized by the personal owner—or rather tenant of the field, and is in consequence to all intent and purpose lost, is nevertheless infinitely great and precious to God. His estimate of its value is for all time expressed in terms of the great Sacrifice, by which alone it is "found"; and by the care with which it is henceforth guarded and increased.

But its chief message is as to the human side. For the Kingdom of Heaven is as it were hidden, and men must make its search the first objective of life. Then when its wealth and all the enrichment and enlargement it promises are realized, there comes the call to sacrifice. Every other interest of life is superseded by its importance; and in that hour eternal issues press for decision. This is surely Christ's correction of the popular error of our own day, that His Gospel is a scheme whereby the maximum good may be secured for the minimum cost. It has been well said of the Kingdom of Heaven that while its entrance fee is nothing, its subscription is all that a man has ! The treasure is without money and without price; and yet we must needs renounce all of self-possession, self-plan, and self-purpose, before it becomes ours. But how great is the satisfaction which transfigures the sacrifice into gladness! For the treasure is absolute, and not merely relative and dependent like those renounced. It enriches life with a new working capital, and makes even ordinary men spiritual millionaires. Let us not fail personally to make it ours. For nothing we may in the alternative gain or keep is comparable.

CHAPTER XIV

" Give ye them to eat " (*v.* 16).

CHRIST'S commands always make conscious our poverty and inability. We may have every desire to serve and bless other lives as we recognize their need, but there is withal a restraining consciousness of insufficiency which checks the impulse and forbids the venture. We know only too well that we have barely sufficient for ourselves. It is in such straits that we may learn the strengthening lesson of His miraculous multiplication of every surrendered resource.

Sincere confession of insufficiency is the first step toward the fulfilment of the command. When the call comes, clear and unmistakable, to carry the Bread of Life to some needy soul, we are at once thrown back upon ourselves. The undertaking is so great that we shrink from it as from some utterly impossible task. And yet He who gives the command knows full well just what are our resources. He is well aware before we tell Him that we have only "five loaves and two fishes." Indeed it is just because we have so little that He calls us to the service; for He designs at the same time both to feed the multitude and to minister to us in such a way as that we shall never again reckon our resources without also reckoning upon Him. For herein lies our great mistake. We have but small and slender provision it is true; but we have HIM! And hence every command of His is a covenanted possibility of sufficiency.

"Bring them hither to Me" must precede the taking of them to the multitude. Even our best and largest things are utterly inadequate, except as they are put in His hand and at His disposal. But then they are transmuted; and from being mere loaves and fishes become the very food of Heaven to those to whom we minister at His bidding. Remember, however, it is always in the breaking of our yielded things that they are multiplied. He gives them back to us—broken for distribution. And when the service is accomplished, and we have given the hungry multitude to eat, we find our own lives have become enriched beyond all thought. It takes indeed twelve baskets to hold the overplus which is the portion of the obedient disciples.

What an honour to dispense Heavenly hospitality with these our own hands !

CHAPTER XV

" *Lord, help me* " (*v.* 25).

IF this is the shortest it is also the strongest prayer of which we have record. When the heart is moved by a sense of profound need, it involuntarily reveals itself. And never so truly as when bowed at the feet of the Lord. We may dissimulate even to the point of deceiving ourselves, as we mingle with men, and compare ourselves by prevalent earthly standards ; but in the presence of Christ every one discloses his true self. Driven by need, and drawn by His sympathy, we come to Him with the assurance that He already knows all about us, and is the only One who can really avail.

For He entirely enters into the burdens which press and the problems which perplex. Are we beset by temptation and harassed by the adversary ? So was He. Are we anxious, as this heathen woman was, for the blessing of those dear to us ? So indeed is He. Do material insecurities and insufficiencies fill us with anxiety ? He had not where to lay His head, and did not possess a penny. Indeed we might traverse the whole range of human experience without touching a single level upon which Christ Himself has not trodden. And hence, when we cry for help, it is to One who fully understands.

Then also faith looks to Him not only as knowing us completely, but as entirely able to help. There is a definiteness about a cry like this which voices a trust in His ability and willingness such as He cannot deny. And though He sometimes subjects our faith to the test of waiting, it is only to give a fuller reward than we asked or thought.

How blessed is the truth that we may have His ear whenever we call, and realize His faithfulness whatever our need ! A thousand times a day I may call in my need—" Lord, help me " ; and just as often as I cry shall I find His power waiting upon my faith.

CHAPTER XVI

" *Some say that Thou art John the Baptist, some Elias, and some Jeremias* " (*v.* 14).

CHRIST'S interest in what men say of Him is simply His interest in them. He is not concerned to win their good opinion, but rather to gain dominion of their hearts and lives. Hence

His query is not an expression of curiosity but of concern ; for right conceptions of Him are essential to right relationship with Him. While the answer here recorded serves to reveal the chaos of men's minds in respect of Him, it does far more. It shows also the perplexing many-sidedness of His character, which at once mystifies and masters those who come to know Him, and is part of His eternal attractiveness.

There is something in Him which identifies Him to various minds with John and Elias and Jeremiah. The wonder is, not that He should be like any one of them in some of the outstanding characteristics of His life and theirs, but that He should be like all three. The plain fact, however, is that all that is good in all other men is seen *in excelsis* in Him. The perfect symmetry of His character in which there is nothing out of proportion proclaims Him, in some degree at least, as the Divine and unique Son of God.

The outstanding characteristic of John's life was his aloofness. He stood apart from the world, manifesting at the same time a disregard and a concern which impressed and drew the multitudes to him, to hear a stern denunciation of sin and a drastic message of repentance.

In the life of Elijah the arresting feature was his authority. Neither king nor priest daunted him in his implacable opposition to idolatry. He stood before God ; and hence had no lack of courage in standing before men, and in calling an entire nation to face the issue and make the choice between worship and wickedness.

Jeremiah was unlike either. The conspicuous quality of his life and ministry was his tenderness. His were the tears of one who loved men, and who brought home to them the message of the everlasting love of God.

Christ united in Himself the strength and quality of all three. The aloofness of John, the authority of Elias, the tenderness of Jeremiah, all combined in Him in such a way as that none could avoid Him, nor mistake His message. The tragedy, however, then and now, is that such recognition of Him should evoke respect and admiration only without faith and love. This is the crowning pathos of His life and ours.

CHAPTER XVII

" No man, save Jesus only " (*v.* 8).

THE Transfiguration was one of the great crises in Christ's life. Up to that time He had been veiled and disguised even to His closest followers. From henceforth the three who shared His nearest intimacy knew Him in an entirely new way, as the Beloved Son of God ;

and got an insight as to His coming death, which, had they always borne in mind, would have saved them much failure in the days to come. For there on the holy mount they saw Christ being strengthened for the final strife and sorrow by an altogether new assurance of the love and good pleasure of the Father.

Moses and Elias are the typical representatives of the Law and the Prophets. They stand for all of moral and spiritual truth which had illumined men and led them Godward previously to the coming of the Lord Christ. Their work was the foreglow of the dawn, the promise of the clear shining of the Light of the world. All that they declared was fulfilled in Him Who was the Antitype of all sacrifice and ordinance, and the Incarnation of all precept and promise. Hence it was that in that hour on the mountain while they faded from the view of the bewildered three, " Jesus only " remained. They, like their work and their authority, vanished from sight when they had handed on to Christ its fulfilment as the last task of His life, to be accomplished only on Calvary. He remained, as He ever will, the solitary Lord of all power and worship.

This then is the watchword of the present as well as the record of the past. To see " no man, save Jesus only " is the open secret of all assured salvation, of all abiding inspiration, of all adequate strength, and of all effective life and

service. For indeed there *is* no other man beside
Him ! Let us then daily climb up above the
dust and din of earth into the mountain of prayer
and fellowship, where we can see Him clearly
and apprehend Him increasingly, as He touches
us and bids us " Arise, and be not afraid." The
whole work of life lies beyond the foot of the hill.
But its success is predetermined there.

CHAPTER XVIII

" *So likewise shall My Heavenly Father do
also unto you* " (*v.* 35).

How much emphasis Christ places upon the
creation and cultivation of right relationship
between men and men. It is as though He
would have us regard it as part of the attestation
of a man's relationship with God, that he is at
peace also with the whole world, and in particular
with his brethren. And it is of striking importance that He makes this a vital part of His
teaching regarding the two most important
things in life—the Divine forgiveness, and the
Divine answering of prayer.

How common is the sin of cherished resentment, and how easy of specious self-justification.
It is never difficult for any one to persuade
himself that intolerable wrong or invasion of
rights has taken place ; when quiet consideration

would often convince him that the injury has been unintentional, the slight unmeant, the wrong merely thoughtless. Christ teaches us to estimate our fellows at their best and not at their worst. His Spirit leads us to credit the highest motive to others, even when their actions seem to be in opposition to our personal interests. For the strong note of His proclamation of the Kingdom is that of brotherhood, with its implicate of mutual love.

But His most insistent emphasis is placed on the fact that any spirit of unforgiveness puts us hopelessly out of touch not only with the one involved, but with God. There is something in a hot, angry heart which makes a man incapable of exercising the simple repentance and faith which condition God's forgiveness. Consequently he remains unblessed. There is something, too, in an implacable and ungracious spirit which strangles true prayer at its very birth. Consequently his prayer is wingless, and never reaches the Throne. May not this be the explanation of many unsatisfied and barren Christian lives? And may not the message of the Gospel to such to-day be the honest and humiliating duty of getting right with others as a necessary preliminary to getting right with God?

CHAPTER XIX

" Go and sell ! Come and follow " (*v.* 21)

WITH unerring skill Christ diagnoses the need, and lays His finger upon the seat of the disorder of every man who comes to Him. His eyes are always aflame with the fire of love, and pierce through every disguise or poise of the soul to its ultimate sincerities. In that realm He judges men by the very message of life which He addresses appropriately to their individual condition ; and which according to their response becomes to them the savour of life unto life or of death unto death.

His demand to the young man who sought of Him the Way of Life is thus to be interpreted and understood. Warm desires, fair record, and keen sensibilities may all exist alongside of some engrossing absorption which cancels the spiritual value of them all. The one thing lacking may in reality be the consequence of something already possessed and loved too well ; and indeed most frequently is. How sincere is the Master in dealing with such an one. He does not lower His standards nor relax the necessary conditions of true life, in order to make it easy for any willingly-embarrassed man to become His disciple. Nor does He ever accommodate Himself to mere human inconveniences. For the realities of the case are altogether too urgent.

Note well the order of His words to the sincere seeker. First "go," and then "come!" The idol must be dethroned by one's own hand. The entanglement must be deliberately cut by the man himself. The determining choice must be made in a moral solitude which no deterring influences are allowed to invade. And this is the supreme test of all. For it searches the sincerity of the inquiring heart, and reveals the reality and depth of every desire after fellowship with the Lord of Life. The alternative and issue is always the same in every age—the world or Christ?

Blessed is the man who comes back to His feet bearing the proceeds of his selling which are henceforth to be consecrated to His use. For he has lost all only to find ALL! But we see here the possibility of a true realization of Christ bringing blight and not blessing, where His dictum is not unhesitatingly obeyed. The greatest of all tragedies is that of the man who goes away, not to sell and then to return and abide, but a sorrowing captive of possessions which have become his possessor.

CHAPTER XX

" Grant that these may sit . . . one on Thy right hand, and the other on Thy left " (*v.* 21).

THIS request on the part of the mother of Zebedee's children is not to be taken as evidence of an entirely ambitious and self-seeking spirit. Had it been prompted by mere desire for prominence, it could not but have met with rebuke. Christ recognized, however, the love toward Himself which was its impulse, and estimated at its true worth the affection of these His friends who longed, not only then, but in the dim future too, to be as close to Him as possible. This is why He does not deny their request; but enunciates the conditions which govern that close fellowship and spiritual power which they seek. The place they desired could only be theirs by an identity with Him in the Cross; and in declaring this He did not seek to dissuade but to enlighten them, lest they should miscalculate the strength of their purpose.

The desire of the loving heart, to live as closely to Christ as is at all possible, is warranted, not merely by the native demands of love, but by the nature also of that holy fellowship. For he who is admitted to the sacred intimacies of close companionship with Him is thereby both inspired in will and empowered in action, and so qualified for service. With such desire, Christ is never at variance.

But those who would sit at His right hand and on His left must needs learn that the way thither is the way of sacrifice. No spiritual advancement is possible except by crucifixion of self, dethronement of self-will, and the utter abandonment of a man's entire being to the will of God. The Cross stands not only for objective truth, but for subjective experience also. It is the only pathway to the highest life of all, a life endued with power to serve and to save.

CHAPTER XXI

" *Go work to-day in My vineyard* " (*v.* 28).

A VITAL part of the Gospel of the Kingdom is its demand for life-service. When a man has entered into assured filial relationship with God, the call inevitably comes to give himself to the work of the vineyard. His response both tests his profession and attests his sincerity. For this call sifts those who hear it, involving as it does the inevitable necessity of a far-reaching choice.

Christ's parable is directed toward our self-discovery in this respect, for it at once proclaims

grace to the repentant man and judgement upon
the insincere. That there is possibility even in
a disobedient life is an outstanding article in
Christ's Evangel, and is here illustrated. The
one who at first bluntly declines to engage in
the service demanded—probably on the score of
the world's attractiveness, the greater freedom
of an unpledged life, or the fancied importance
of some already-made engagement—ultimately
repents. Nor is it difficult to estimate some at
least of the influences which brought him to
a worthier frame of mind. The grief of his
father, the unchecked uprising of a sense of duty,
the discovery of an inner inexplicable incom-
pleteness, all contributed toward his victory
over that natural disinclination to openly reverse
a former wilfulness, of which we all know something. But "he repented and went," and found
the work still awaiting him! The fact is that
God seldom if ever gets more from any of us
than the belated obedience of repentance, for
few obey His first call. How great is the grace
which accepts this, and does not forbid us the
field!

On the other hand the merely sentimental
recognition of responsibility of the one who says,
"I go, sir, and went not," leads to permanent
self-exclusion. To say "Lord, Lord," without
doing the will of the Father, is of all sins the
most inexcusable. Knowledge which is not

converted into obedient service is the heaviest
condemnation which can rest upon any man.
Therefore, " go work to-day ; " for to-morrow
is coming, and with it the judgement.

CHAPTER XXII

" *They made light of it* " (*v.* 5).

THE spirit of unconscious trifling is apt to
grow upon men until some crisis reveals the
moral dry-rot which has, all unsuspected, been
going on. These men in the parable certainly
did not begin by slightingly rejecting the invitation of a King. The trifling habit had grown
upon them, and this was their self-revealing
crisis. The Gospel does not urge solemnity of
manner upon men ; but it does urge seriousness
of mind, without which men may lose themselves
eternally, even though so close to the promises
and power of God.

The subject-matter of the proffered excuses
is too worthless for consideration. For what
are a farm and merchandise in comparison with
the things of the Kingdom of Heaven ? They
may, of course, be made into excuses by the
insincere and unwilling man, but can never be
seriously set forth as reasons for the rejection
of the Divine invitation. The fact is, however,
that these things are constantly increasing their

grip upon the lives of those who willingly yield
themselves to them, until they cannot be shaken
off. Possessions are apt to become the master
of the one who makes them the chief end of his
life; until, when challenged by some demands
of the Son of God, they flame into hot and fierce
revolt. Few, if any, set out with the considered
intention of meriting the wrath of God by doing
despite to His Gospel. But to such lengths as
these does habitual light-hearted trifling with
eternal things bring men.

Let us be seriously on our guard against this
besetting danger. For to yield to any spirit
which treats the precepts and promises of God
as things of little moment, which may be carelessly neglected now in the vain hope that in
any future time of need they may be turned to,
is the pathway of disaster. For God will not
wait for ever upon our convenience; nor can we
trifle with Him save at our own peril.

CHAPTER XXIII

*"How often would I . . . and ye would
not"* (*v.* 37).

CHRIST'S lament over Jerusalem follows hard
upon His denunciation of those who professed
to be the religious leaders and teachers of His
day. His sternest words were pronounced against

the men who while ostensibly living in the light
of truth so entirely opposed the Truth Incarnate.
For their spirit and attitude had not unnaturally
communicated itself to the whole people, pre-
disposing them to reject Him as He announced
His mission of salvation. Such is the outcome
of the influence which we constantly exert one
upon another, and its serious responsibility.

" *How often would I ?* "—What a revelation
these words afford of the heart of Christ in its
yearning solicitude to bless even the thankless
and ungracious. It is as though again and again
He had looked out upon those who were defenceless and in danger, as chicks from a bird of prey,
and had longed to shelter and save them. This
is the interpretation of all His loving invitations
which had fallen on unheeding ears. And yet
despite the ingratitude and heedlessness with
which it was received, the warmth of His love
was not chilled. His " how often " speaks of
a boundless tenderness and pity, which even the
unwillingness of men could not destroy.

" *And ye would not.*"—It is on this account
that every ill from which Christ could have
delivered comes upon them. For it is a certainty
that He can do nothing for us except as we are
willing He should. Faith in Him is not a mere
assent of the mind, but a consent also of the will.
And if any of us is unblessed, the cause of our
condition is to be sought not in Him but in

ourselves. " What wouldest thou that I should
do unto thee ? " is always the Saviour's query.
Alas ! that He should so often have to say to us,
as of Jerusalem, that having opened His heart
to us and called us to Himself we " would not."

CHAPTER XXIV

" *Be ye also ready* " (*v.* 44).

NOTHING is clearer in the whole range of
Christ's teaching regarding the future than the
certainty of His coming, and the uncertainty
also of its time. Indeed it is a vital and integral
part of His Gospel that He is to return, and
that His coming again will mean for His people
the completion and consummation of the
blessing which has come to them by His first
appearing. That His people have in this our
day very largely lost sight of this fact which
should be their inspiring hope, is one of the
results of the spirit of worldliness which has been
allowed to invade His Church. For when men's
hearts are absorbed in present engrossments and
fastened upon material good, they are disinclined
to hail with gladness the tidings of the great
Event which will mean the interruption of all
that goes to make up the gladness and glory of
their life. And yet the truth is plain and unmistakable, and the warning of the Saviour indubit-

ably clear. The one unmistakable certainty of the future which is otherwise so largely hidden from us, is that Christ is to come again, and that without warning. His exhortation to readiness is in reality the sum total of His ethic.

For what does it mean to be thus ready for His return ? Not the neglect of ordinary duty nor the unfulfilment of common responsibility, in favour of any exercise falsely regarded as more spiritual. Into this error not a few have fallen, to the utter discredit of the whole glorious truth of His return. Rather does it mean the elevation of all these things into the service of His Kingdom. For it is as servants we are bidden to watch for our Lord, and as those who are doing His will, that we shall recognize Him.

Is our life of such quality that we are unashamedly ready to continue it in His immediate presence ? Do we love His appearing because we love Him supremely ?

CHAPTER XXV

" Inasmuch as ye have done it unto one of the least of these My brethren, ye have done it unto Me " (v. 40).

This is a part of the Saviour's parable of the human brotherhood. As the Son of Man, He identified Himself with all need, claimed all love, and judged all selfishness. On the one hand He accepts every service lovingly rendered to the poor, the hungry, the sick, the sad, as offered to Himself. On the other hand He rebukes every selfishness which withholds and withdraws from human need, as being the expression of a hostile attitude toward Him. And at the same time He lifts a corner of the veil which hides eternity from our view, and reveals the ultimate issues of both earth's love and selfishness. That His words should equally surprise the rewarded and the rejected is not strange, for neither is conscious of the real weight and worth of doings which have become habitual, until they hear Him say "Ye did it unto Me," or "Ye did it not unto Me."

Such words as these invest all our contacts with the world with new meaning. For they proclaim that everything in life gains in value or sinks to worthlessness according to its relationship to His central government. And this ideal of living in all things as unto Christ is in itself an uplift and an inward impulse. For life without such ennobling inspiration is apt to degenerate into the material and the sordid. To regard it, however, as an earthly opportunity for the fulfilment of heavenly obligation is to give it wings wherewith to soar into the clear atmosphere of fellowship with Him, and wherewith to speed to the service of the needy and oppressed. To know that little things may be done by us in the same spirit of consecration in which others have accomplished great things, lends new hopefulness to the weary and often disheartened worker.

It is possible for the loftiest love to be seen shining in beauty in the heart of the lowliest deed; and we may be certain that whoever fails to recognize it there, He for whom it is intended will not miss it when at the close of the day He reckons with His servants.

CHAPTER XXVI

" Sleep on now, and take your rest " (*v.* 45).

CHRIST'S closest disciples and most trusted friends failed Him in the very heart of His life's crisis. In the last great struggle of His soul, He sought the aid of human intercourse. He Who had poured out His own love so freely sought for Himself some heartening cordial of human devotion as He entered upon the agony in the Garden. How pathetic and tragic is it, that in that hour when all was darkest and hardest He should be disappointed. What a heart-piercing rebuke did these words of His convey to them in that hour of His victory which was so soon to look like utter defeat. " Sleep on now! the hour of your great opportunity,

and of My great need, has gone never to return.
Sleep on now ! as long and as soundly as you
may, you have missed your chance of ministering to Me. The good angels have embraced it,
and have done what you might have done.
Sleep on now, and take your rest ! "

He was not ironical in that hour of IIis disciples' failure. He spoke out of a broken heart,
crushed by disappointment and sad for the men
who had themselves lost what Eternity could
never recover to them. And so He bids them
sleep on, for their slumber now does not matter.
However wakeful they may now become, they
cannot regain their lost opportunity. For the
future, however carefully guarded, never atones
nor makes up for the neglect of past days.
Such a loss of opportunity as this must be
eternal.

The history of most of our failures is the
history of similar neglected or unrecognized
opportunities. The hour which is big with
some crisis of fate usually looks just like one
of the ordinary hours of the day, and gives no
hint of its greatness. The disguise of the
commonplace tests both our powers of percep-
tion and our readiness of action. But invariably
we awaken to our loss sooner or later, for Christ
loves us too well to have it otherwise. All life's
" might have beens " never fail to come back
to us, and to unite in speaking this bitter con-

demnation—" Sleep on now and take your
rest." We get to know when it is too late that
Christ has been asking us to watch with Him,
and that we have preferred our case.

CHAPTER XXVII

" *A crown of thorns* " (*v.* 29).

THE plaited thorns was merely a rough jest
of the brutal soldiery who were making merry
over the contrast between Christ and Caesar. It
was just their way of expressing contempt for
One whose professions of Kingship were so
utterly contradicted by His condition. They
could not understand how any one so defenceless
and weak should seriously put forward such
claims. So they crowned Him in mocking derision,
making a rough coronet of thorn-twigs, and
placing it with laughing scorn upon His brow.

But in doing so they were acting more appropriately and symbolically than they were themselves capable of knowing. For the crown of
thorns was in reality the only fitting crown of
Christ's life. Other crowns He had already
refused. This one He silently accepted and
wore. For it spoke to Him of the curse which
He lifted and bore for all men. It expressed all
the poignancy of human sorrow which He shared
and carried for the whole race. It fittingly

symbolized the disguised glory of a life of suffering and sacrifice. And it has become His imperishable honour. Indeed it is by the cross of shame which He made His throne, and the crown of thorns which He wore as His diadem, that He has always conquered and swayed the hearts of sinful men. Here His " love so amazing, so Divine " is seen at its fairest and fullest.

While, however, the crown of thorns has become one of the marks to lead men to Him, telling as it does of His unspeakable sacrifice, it reminds us also of the awful potency of our sin. For what the Roman soldiers did, we too may do. We may crown and crucify Him afresh by our practical rejection of His claims, by our heedlessness of His calls, by our trifling or serious indifference to His love. We may dishonour Him as they did in an hour of sinful mirth, to our eternal shame. Yet even then His love will continue to flow out towards us; and His crown of thorns will still declare His saving grace.

CHAPTER XXVIII

" Lo ! I am with you alway " (*v.* 20).

In many respects this, Christ's last word, is His greatest. For it promises that all His disciples had already known Him to be, and had experienced in Him, should be amplified. The perfect understanding and sympathy, the sure guidance and inspiration, the miraculous power of defence and deliverance which had blessed them during those hallowed days, they were henceforth to know not in part but fully, and not merely occasionally as hitherto but always. It assured them of adequate co-operation in their every moral endeavour to carry out His bidding, and promised a victory which otherwise had been but an impossible dream. Indeed, the history of the Christian Church in every subsequent age has been simply the unfolding of this proclamation. All the upbuilding, extension, and progress of the Kingdom has been due to the abiding presence of the King.

Note that this word is not absolute but contingent. It is indissolubly linked with the command to " Go into all the world and preach the Gospel to every creature." Its life-giving experience can only be known by those who are actually endeavouring to obey the call to herald the Evangel. Failure in consciousness of His nearness, which we often deplore, is usually traceable directly or indirectly to failure in strenuous and whole-souled service. For this is not a promise, but a fact. Whatever happens He *is* with His people in unconditioned love. But the degree of their realization of Him, with all that it means, is entirely dependent upon their personal obedience.

Further, Christ is not to be called upon in any of life's emergencies, if He is neglected when no special occasion for His help is recognized. He must be enthroned and obeyed " all the days," if we would have Him consciously near when the danger is imminent and the need immediate. Every day is *the* great day of life to His disciples. For every day He is at hand.

St. MARK

CHAPTER I

" Forthwith, when they were come out of the synagogue, they entered into the house " (*v.* 29).

This Gospel is peculiarly the record of the servant of God. Foretold in prophecy, both in outline and detail, the ideal life of Divine service, with all its governing attitudes of obedience, self-forgetfulness, loyalty and love, is fulfilled only in Christ. From this angle of vision the second Evangelist caught the revelation of the Lord; and, throughout, his is the presentation of the holy activities of His earthly days in His contacts with the burdens and problems of men. Other inspired writers may dwell on His unique relationship to the Father, upon the synagogue aspects of His life. Mark's abiding impressions are of His entering into the house, and His manifestation there of the power which fellowship and intimacy with God bestows.

The synagogue and the house! How entirely is the Christian life comprehended in this twofold aspect. Worship and work, contemplation and action, meditation and mediation make up for all of us life's whole content. And their interaction is clear and unmistakable. It is in

the synagogue that we learn Heaven's secrets.
It is in the house, with its humdrum duties, its
recurrent needs, and its monotonous round, that
we proceed to prove their dynamic strength.
The only effective preparation for life is regularly
and frequently to keep tryst with the Lord in
some synagogue of His appointment. And the
only worthy outcome of the blessing of those
sacred hours is in close and patient application
to the work of some house, also of His appointment.

To bring the odour of the Holiest, of "myrrh,
aloes, and cassia," into the atmosphere of the
common-place, is to follow Christ in the plan
and pattern of His life-work.

CHAPTER II

" *It was noised that He was in the house* "
(*v.* 1).

WHEREVER Christ went it was the same. His
presence could never be mistaken, nor His
influence avoided. Whether it is into the house
at Capernaum, or into the habitation of any
human heart that He comes, the fact that He is
present is attested by what happens there. For
there are indubitable evidences that a new force
is at work, that a new order is inaugurated, and
that a new government is established; and

they are of the sort that all men recognize. Nor could it be otherwise since He is the very Lord of all power.

What are to be regarded as such evidences of His incoming? To mention but a few, there is, first of all, the adoption of His attitude of both separation and contact in regard to the world. For His indwelling power at once expels all mere worldly loves, and inspires life with a passion to bless the world by bringing to it the saving Word. Then there is also an acknowledgement of His ownership; not in any mere theological but in a sternly practical way. For He abides in the house entirely upon the terms of obedience, and only as we do whatsoever He says. Further, there is a growing approximation to His likeness, and a reflection of His character in the simple graces of unselfishness, purity, generosity, and love for which all life's duties supply a perfect screen. These are amongst the commonest things which silently—and yet how loudly !—proclaim to the beholding world that He is in the house.

Once this is noised abroad He never fails to attract the hungry, eager, wistful worldlings to Himself. The surrendered life becomes His medium of display, and the scene of a saving and healing work, in which the glory is so entirely His that the mere house which He thus honours is made for ever obscure.

CHAPTER III

" That they should be with Him, and that He might send them forth " (*v.* 14).

THE call to holy intimacy with Christ by no means ended with its acceptance by the Twelve. Its echoes have reverberated down all the ages, assuring His people of His purpose, admitting them into His fellowship, and commissioning them to His service. Every extension of the Kingdom has had its beginnings in some heart-response to this invitation ; and its significance is yet unexhausted.

" That they should be with Him."—This is at once the purpose and the preparation of the disciple. To be " with " Christ means much more than to live in mere physical proximity to Him. It expresses union of will and life, the sympathy of a man's entire moral being with the aim and intent of the Saviour. It is, in short, His own antithesis of being " against Him." Then, to the one whose decision has been recorded by a forsaking of every other attraction, this word gives the secret of the only effective qualification for the duties of the life embraced. Companionship with Him alone makes His people courageous to carry out His programme. In the secret place they learn what are His

resources—and theirs. At His feet their faults
are corrected, their character formed, and their
hearts inspired. Thus by being with Him they
are endued to go forth for Him and to represent
all that He stands for in a world of sin and
sorrow. Nor is there any other way of fitness.

"*That He might send them forth.*"—They do
not rush hither and thither in mere haphazard
search of service. Each has his own particular
appointment both as to his field and his fellow-
servant. And each has the steadying consciousness that he is doing the will of his Lord—
nothing less, nothing more, and nothing else. In
days of disappointment and difficulty his heart
never doubts but that he is fulfilling a trust,
and so he faints not. And when at the end of the
long day He calls His disciples once again to Him,
that they may be with Him to go out no more for
ever, each one shall then know in the fulness of
his reward how great has been the importance of
his own bit of work, as part of the Eternal plan.

CHAPTER IV

"When the sun was up, it was scorched" (*v.* 6).

THIS is one of the most significant instances
of Christ's discriminating characterization of the
hearers of the Word. It stands for those who
" receive it with gladness," but who having no

depth of character are incapable of any depth
of conviction. In consequence, when the first
flood of emotion has ebbed, and the opposition
in which loyalty to the truth always involves
men arises, it finds them without any strength
of resistance; and as they wilt and wither they
become a reproach to the cause they have
professed.

The severest condemnation which any man
ever incurs is that he endures " but for a time."
For continuance is always the proof of reality
in whatever sphere the effort be made. Christian
profession is in the nature of the case inevitably
exposed to the fierce heat-rays of the world-sun.
If its roots of faith do not strike down deep into
the soil of truth, and firmly entwine there around
the central verities from whence sustaining rich-
ness is alone to be drawn, it cannot but fade.
And this is to fail indeed of the grace of God, and
to involve His reputation as the heavenly Hus-
bandman. The world is always ready to point
with scorn at those who do not fulfil the early
promise of their declared purpose ; and there is
indeed nothing which so adversely affects Christ's
cause as the case of such. Hence our personal
responsibility for the deepening of our own lives.

There is a promise of the Lord which every one
who is exposed to this common danger may
plead. It is that the sun, however fierce its rays,
" shall not smite thee by day." And it implies

that the cooling rain and dew from heaven make
it possible not only to withstand the scorching
heat, but to derive also positive good from it.
Even in the hottest and dustiest days lives so
sustained will be fresh and fragrant witnesses to
His power.

CHAPTER V

" Go home to thy friends and tell them "
(v. 19).

This must surely be the outcome of every
saving contact with Christ. When He has
cleansed and liberated any man from the stain
and bondage of sin, He makes him a potential
witness to those who cannot refute his testimony,
nor fail to appreciate the change wrought in him.
It is written large over all experience of His
grace as one of its immutable laws, that no man
liveth unto himself.

Christ's concern in this instance is twofold.
First, He wants to bring the man himself into
the fullest blessing and largest life. It is on
this account that He commissions him to a
service in which both his own assurance shall
deepen and his latent powers shall be developed
and secured for the Kingdom. For He sees in
a poor saved demoniac a possible ambassador!
The remnant of a life so long lived under evil

sway is not without glorious possibility in the
eyes of Christ. He redeems this man and all
others also from destruction unto devotion. Nor
is His work complete until, inspired by grateful
love, He has set the saved one on the pathway
of a service in which he shall both find himself
and accomplish the purpose of the Lord.

Then, also, Christ's love yearns over those
unblessed ones whom this man may reach in
a way quite impossible to any other. For their
need is no less than was his, although it is not
expressed in the same form ; and it can be met
in only the same way, by the healing touch of
the Saviour. So his experience is to become his
Evangel, in the sphere where he is best known,
and where on that very account the difficulties
are greatest. But the Saviour's command to
return thither, itself carries the implicate of His
own co-operation. The unseen Master goes with
His servant to share the toil and multiply its
result.

CHAPTER VI

" *Come ye yourselves apart—and rest a
while* " (*v.* 31).

How great is Christ's solicitude for His
servants ! He Who so often sought the healing
solitudes for Himself, shared their secret with
His weary and burdened friends, that they too

might learn the recreative power of undisturbed fellowship with God. For in the desert, free from the distractions of ordinary life and duty, men are the better able to hold communion with Him Who speaks to their hearts most clearly when other voices are silenced.

Amid the busy rush of our modern life how necessary it is that we should frequently seek the seclusion of His presence. For in the throng and press we are in danger of losing that elevation of motive and purpose which conditions all worthy discipleship, and of becoming mechanical alike in our piety and practice. Then, too, exhaustion of strength makes long continuance upon the highest levels almost impossible, except as we are renewed by regenerating contacts with the Lord. Indeed, it is not too much to say that every peril which besets busy lives would be avoided did we but respond to those wooing invitations of the Master to the fellowship of the desert-place with the same loving delight as in which He extends them. For there, as our hearts are opened to Him, He can correct our mistaken estimates, renew our expended energies, illumine our beclouded minds, and reassure our discouraged hearts. And of all these ministries we stand in need.

This age of ours is full of restlessness. Activity is apt to expand, and meditation to contract to dangerous limits. Purposeful withdrawal to

commune with Christ is the only antidote to its
deadly feverishness.   And it is adequate and
available to us all.

CHAPTER VII

" *For from within, out of the heart of men,
proceed . . .*" (*vv.* 21–2).

Of what sort is the effluence of our lives?
This is the certain test of the profession of our
lips.   For it reveals unerringly the hidden man
of the heart, which is the real man in every one
of us.   This is the primary objective of all
Christ's teaching—to reveal men to themselves.
His first work is always to create and quicken
that self-consciousness without which there can
never be any true consciousness of God.   For
it is only as the knowledge of indwelling sin
becomes a pressing certainty that men incline
toward submission to the saving and delivering
power of the Lord.   Conviction and contrition
must of necessity precede confession and
cleansing.

Habits and actions reveal disposition.   " As
a man thinketh in his heart, so is he."   Crises,
whether of good or evil opportunity, do not
make a man.   They simply serve to disclose
him.   None of us is ever really surprised into
any of the grosser forms of sin.   Onlookers may

be surprised at us, but we are not ourselves surprised. For we know full well the secret process which has been going on. The final fall has been long delayed it may be; but it was all along inevitable.

It is full of significance that the first of this terrifying catalogue of sins of which Christ speaks is " evil thoughts." In the thought-life every unholiness has its birth ; and it is hence there that the control of Christ must be manifested if His Salvation is to be effective in any life. The secret of all pure and worthy effluence, which is indeed nothing less than the Spirit of God flowing from the inner man as " rivers of living water," is only reached by daily yielding the whole government of life to the Lord Christ. He alone can keep our thoughts from ranging over forbidden fields; and can inspire a love of " whatsoever things are pure and lovely, and of good report," which ensures our thinking on these things. Thus, and in no other way, is the well-spring of any life sweetened, and its effluence assured.

CHAPTER VIII

" Whosoever will come after Me . . . let him take up his cross and follow Me " (v. 34).

CHRIST loves men far too well to hide from them the cost and consequence of discipleship. He never veils the hardness of the way, nor tones down the moral requirement, in order to gain allegiances. Indeed it would almost seem as though He deliberately planned to drive some men away, while drawing others to Him. For the fact is that throughout His earthly life, as now, His Word both wins and winnows, sifts and saves those who hear it. The day on which a man is brought face to face with His call and claim is his judgement day.

The Cross signifies to the disciple just what it signified to the Master. It is not a mere picturesque description of a hard lot, a restricting infirmity, or a personal insufficiency, as is often mistakenly thought. In His life it stood for the last malignant expression of the world's hostility. From the very outset the world " knew Him not." As He toiled and travailed for its blessing, the only response He met was rejection and scorn, which intensified as He drew near to the end, and eventually culminated in the Cross. And He plainly declares that to live in fellowship with Him involves a man in the same hostile treatment at the hands of the same world. The testimony of a life which brings God before the consciousness of those who deliberately plan to live as though He were not, cannot but meet with rejection. For it convicts men of selfishness and sin as nothing else can do. The hostility of the world to Christ and His disciples is deep rooted in human pride.

We are not to shun, nor yet seek to avoid this outcome of loyal faith. Still less are we to make a cross for ourselves. The Master enjoins patient submission, and bids us " take " up its burden as He did. For the influence of every such cross-bearing life is redemptive. Only by those who follow His steps can the world be blessed, and His purpose of salvation be realized.

CHAPTER IX

" If the salt have lost his saltness ! " (v. 50).

CHRIST's warnings are a vital part of His Gospel. He who " knew what was in man " is always aware of the possibility of failing purpose, waning energy, and actual defection; and does not fail to declare their danger to His followers. By virtue alone of their union with Him they are to exercise an influence upon the world like that of salt—preventive, preservative, and purifying. Should that vital union, however, become impaired from any cause, this essential quality is lost, and their life becomes utterly worthless.

Salt may lose its saltness from one of two causes. As every housewife knows, if it is brought into contact with certain other substances, it yields its properties and becomes insipid. Just so is it with the Christian life. Its peculiar influence is inevitably forfeited by voluntary contact with things actually condemned or morally doubtful. Positive sin and self-indulgence of course admit of no question in this respect. More subtle, but not less strong in its destructive power, is the spirit of worldliness, which, at first reluctant and half-afraid, becomes tolerant and self-excusing, then casuistically self-justifying, and is ultimately accepted as the normal standard of life without protest. It is in this way that many a disciple has deteriorated into actual worthlessness. On the other hand, salt may lose its saltness by failure of contact. Such is its nature that it only saves its life by imparting it ; and if kept alone it strangely forfeits its essential qualities. So also is the Christian life. Only by such contacts with the sin and need of the world as are effected by witnessing, soul-winning, and un-selfish service can it maintain its own powers. Most serious, too, is the fact that such a process

of loss may go on all unconsciously, until some
outstanding occasion reveals the deterioration
which cannot be atoned for. For there is really
no answer to the Master's query, " wherewith ? "

CHAPTER X

" *For even the Son of Man came not to be
ministered unto, but to minister* " (*v.* 45).

How essentially different to ordinary conceptions of greatness is Christ's ideal. The world
looks upon that man as great who is able to
command the service of others. Christ is the
eternal example of the greatness of the sincere
servant. The only one of His sayings which is
unrecorded in the Gospels but given to us else-
where, might well be taken as the motto of
His life—" It is more blessed to give than to
receive." For it was in this spirit, and with this
joy set before Him, that He lived and died. And
it is this principle and purpose of life which He
commends to those who follow Him.

How indiscriminate He was in the exercise
of this ministry. It is comparatively easy to
serve those who are thankful and responsive in
their appreciation. The warm glow of their
gratitude is at once a compensation and an

inspiration. But when motives are misconstrued, efforts suspected, and gifts but grudgingly received—if accepted at all, it is hard indeed to continue cheerfully to seek the good of the churlish and unappreciative. And yet He did. Never did any one receive less encouragement than that with which His efforts were met. Never was generous love so despised, nor selfless service so spurned. And never was beneficent purpose so entirely victorious in its independence of the adventitious stimulus of thanks. Had it been otherwise, the mighty work of the world's salvation had never been wrought.

The secret of such a life as this, which it must be remembered is not only our propitiation but our pattern also, is in the fact that Christ regarded Himself as having no rights, except the right to serve. There was no conflict in Him between the call of opportunity and the claim of dignity. Surrender to the will of the Father had for ever settled that; while a constant outlook upon the world-need inspired His ceaseless activity. If we would follow Him in such a life, we must first follow Him to the place of surrender, which is also the mount of vision. And He has shown us the pathway thither.

CHAPTER XI

" *Nothing but leaves* " (*v.* 13).

IN nothing does Christ so severely condemn the inconsistent and discrepant life of fruitless profession as in this miracle. The actual is obviously invested with the symbolical; and the lesson enjoined by that destructive action amid the solemn circumstances of the last week of His earthly life is full of significance. We are apt to forget the darkness of the terror of the Lord, in the light of His tenderness. The fact that on His way to the Cross He could pause to pronounce such a doom upon the worthless tree, should persuade and stimulate our memory to full apprehension of His perfect character.

It is of the nature of the fig-tree to produce its blossom and fruit before its foliage. Hence the raising of Christ's expectation, and His disappointment. As a picture of profession without piety, and of creed without character, its likeness is self-evident. For there are many whose lives it unerringly represents. Christ comes to them hungering at heart for some fruit of their faith in the form of practical love toward Him, of self-sacrificing service for Him, of supreme desire for His glory. And He is disappointed and saddened at finding none of these things. The leaves of religious observance, or external worship, of correct theology, are all there in luxuriant abundance. But He Who searches hearts looks behind and beyond these for the one attestation of true discipleship—fruit. Without this all else is less than worthless, for it partakes of the nature of hypocrisy, which is of all sins the most deadly.

Note the significance of the punishment of worthlessness. That which does not fulfil the Divine purpose dies. There is a sin of omission which can only lead to the withdrawal of opportunity, and the forfeiture of life. This is the full force of Christ's acted parable, which voices to us all the plainest and tenderest warnings of the love of God.

CHAPTER XII

" Jesus sat over against the treasury " (*v.* 41).

OF all the realms of Christian duty that of giving is most frequently invaded and characterized by a spirit of haphazard carelessness. Even where responsibility is to a degree acknowledged, the actual matter of our gifts both as to their proportion and direction is too often a mere matter of thoughtless impulse, or a casual following of the lead of others. On this account much that is cast into the coffers of God's house is without any real worth; for it is always motive which determines value. How different

would our giving be if we realized that Jesus
sits over against the treasury, to scrutinize the
offerers and to appraise their offerings !

His keen eyes of love are indifferent to the
ordinary standards by which men compute
values. The gifts of the rich are but fragments
of their abundance. The mites of the poor
widow are a true offering, and are set forth as
exceeding in preciousness all else that has been
cast in. There are some copper coins which
shine with a lustre and beauty that mere gold
ones never acquire ; for they are burnished by
the love they represent. In the Saviour's sight
they are both potentially and actually worth far
more than all that has been given by mere force
of custom or convention. And His esteem is
all that matters, both now and eternally.

He measures the extent of all gifts by a twofold standard. Firstly, how much calculated
sacrifice they represent. No one offers his whole
living to the Lord except as the result of a careful
estimation of His claims in comparison with
every other interest. And only the great love
of one who has been much forgiven is sufficient
inspiration for this. Then, also, He looks at
how much is left when the gift has been made.
This is the searching test which determines His
opinion of our offerings. Are they actually
representative of the surrender of the entire
possession of life, or they are but a pittance in

comparison with the larger overplus which we regard as our own? For their proportion unerringly records the esteem in which we hold Him.

CHAPTER XIII

"*When ye shall see the abomination of desolation . . . flee to the mountains*" (*v.* 14).

THERE is a place of refuge for the people of God when all around them is in chaos. The march of events sooner or later brings stern tests to faith, when overwhelmed and over-powered hearts are prone to ask if God has forgotten to be gracious. Dark clouds gather, and every prospect is filled with anxiety. The very foundations of life at such times seem to be removing, and the righteous are sore troubled in uncertainty as to what to do. Under these circumstances, from which none of us can entirely escape, the only available and sufficient resource is in communion with God. When the smoke of battle fills the valleys so that we can discern nothing clearly, then we must betake us to the mountain. For there the air is clear and the view unhindered. From thence we can look out on life without fearfulness. And there is renewed our confidence in God's faithfulness, as the ultimate security of our lives.

This injunction Christ exemplified in His own

life. To study His bearing under the trials of disappointment, stress, and seeming failure, in the days when He saw the "abomination of desolation" all around Him, is to learn the true inwardness of this word. For He was ever betaking Himself to the mountain, that in fellowship with the Father He might be reinvigorated for life amid the scenes of sin and sorrow. And this is the only way of power for us all.

It is no counsel of cowardice which Christ enjoins when He says "flee." It often takes courage of a higher order to face God than to face life—especially when the "abomination of desolation" is the direct consequence of personal sin. At such times the mountain has its terrors beyond anything that the plain holds ; and on its heights the sorest controversy of all must be settled. But it is in the adjustment and cultivation of relationship with Heaven that we are alone prepared to shed light upon the darkness of that other land in which our days must be passed.

CHAPTER XIV

"Where is My guest-chamber?" (v. 14, R.V.).

THE significant meaning of this question which Christ directed to His anonymous disciple in the city of Jerusalem is by no means exhausted in its reference to Him. It is just an illustration

of the Saviour's reiterated desire for the possession of the lives of His professed people; and of
a true man's consecration.

Christ is always saying to us : " If you believe
in Me, you belong to Me. If you believe that
I have redeemed you with My precious Blood,
then yield to Me the life which is rightly Mine.
Give Me My crown rights as your King, Who
am your King because I am first your Saviour."
This is the real meaning of the demand which
comes to us again and again. " Where is My
guest-chamber ? " And our answer is the
record of the reality or unreality of our faith.
It is the one who gives to Him the guest-
chamber, the highest and supremest place in
heart and life, and who holds all that he is and
has as a sacred trust for the use of the Master,
who is a true Christian.

Christ's acceptance and use of this guest-
chamber shows that its owner had done an
infinitely bigger thing than he had conceived
when he gave it up to the use of the Master.
One moment it was but the ordinary guest-room
of a Jewish house. The next it was the throne-
room of the King of kings. In that room the
Lord Jesus took the common cups and plates
which formed part of its furnishing, and made
them the vessels of the First Sacrament.

To that same room also He came again after
His resurrection, and from thence He sent

His disciples into all the world to preach the
Gospel. Upon them, as they gathered there
after His departure, He sent the Spirit at
Pentecost. That room became the most God-
used room the world has ever known. So, too,
it is with our lives. Christ takes that which we
yield to Him, and multiplies its use beyond
anything we have thought possible. No offer
is regarded as too unworthy or small, if only
it is full and complete. No guest-chamber is
offered to Him with all the honesty of a loving
heart which He does not accept, and occupy,
and use.

CHAPTER XV

"He saved others; Himself He cannot save"
(*v. 31*).

THIS mocking taunt of Christ's foes has
become the triumphant Evangel of His friends.
It was meant to express contempt for His
weakness as He hung upon the Cross. In reality
it proclaims His power for all time. For it
declares the governing principle of every redemptive force. Blessing to others can only flow
through an entirely unselfish life. Salvation is
ever the fruit of sacrifice. A life laid down is
always the price at which lives are lifted up.
He Who saved others cannot save Himself. In

this His enemies spoke more truly than they were aware.

How unerringly do all the temporary and local events of the Saviour's supreme sacrifice set forth His unspeakable love! Every incident is like a lens which brings more clearly into view the glory of His patience, His tenderness, and His humility. The power of the Godhead is never seen in such greatness as when so restrained; and nothing exhibits Christ's ability to save men to the uttermost as does His voluntary inability to save Himself. Its brightness outshone and darkened the sun. Its message dispels every sin-born fear. It is His eternal attractiveness to stained and maimed men.

And in this, as in all things, Christ is the Example and Forerunner of His people. They, too, cannot save others, except as they are willing to lose their own lives. Each redeemed man is as a corn of wheat. He may "abide alone" if he will, living for himself and seeking mainly his own good; until every undeveloped possibility rises up to condemn him for ever. Or he may " bring forth much fruit," by yielding himself to God for the service of others. And it is to this use of life that the Saviour inspires all who follow Him. What a record for any man's enemies to be compelled to declare of him : " He saved others " !

CHAPTER XVI

"*He appeared in another form*" (*v.* 12).

AMONGST the many great declarations of the Resurrection, none is more significant than that of Christ's unrestricted power of appearance and approach to men. Hitherto in the days of His flesh He bore one sacred form which did not vary. Now He is no longer confined in any national, or local, or social characteristic. In His risen life He who is indispensable to the life of all men, appears and appeals to them according to their widely differing circumstances. His power of self-revelation is henceforth illimitable, and to every man according to his need He declares Himself.

This is the explanation of the innumerable variety of men's experience of Him. Some get to know Him in one way, some in another, just as in the day of His rising again. Some of His disciples come to know Him as the Living One in the garden; some through the fellowship of the upper-room; some in the toil of their calling on the sea-shore; and others in the intercourse of the common highway. So it has ever been. But the truth is, that though He appears in varying forms it is always with unvarying meaning. His purpose is unchanged, though

His presence may be disguised ; for it is always
to heal, to help, to hearten, and to hallow that
He draws near. There are twelve gates to the
City, and every one is a pearl.

The greatest tragedy of life is, that mere
second causes should be allowed to hide Him.
For He comes in every promise of new hope,
every dawning of new ideal, every imperative
of new duty, every stress of new temptation,
and every bitterness of new sorrow. And He
is Himself the interpretation of each. Let us
not miss Him as He assumes " another form "
than that in which we have always conceived
Him, lest we fail of the *manifold* wisdom and
grace of God.

St. LUKE

CHAPTER I

" Great in the sight of the Lord " (*v.* 15).

THIS prophetic description of Christ's fore-runner is at once a comprehensive record of his life, and a pattern also for the lives of all those who in any way seek to prepare the way of the Lord. Greatness is a matter about which there exists much misconception, for men's standards by which it is measured vary considerably. There are a thousand things of attainment, achievement, and possession which are commonly regarded as evidences of greatness; but which in the light of Eternity are merely deco-rated littleness. To be "great in the sight of the Lord" is, after all, the only greatness which matters, for it alone endures.

John the Baptist was great in the utter sincerity of his consecration to the will of God. The rugged. prophet of the desert, with his scorn of the merely superficial and conventional, stands out boldly as one who never counted the cost to himself of entire faithfulness. The petty honours of the world, its fleeting smiles and frowns, concerned him not at all. A whole-souled purpose of fulfilling his mission and of declaring the Word of God to a forgetful people dominated him. His asceticism was that which must ever characterize the one who lives amid heavenly realities while dwelling among earthly needs. True greatness is a compact of utter independence and unmixed integrity.

John was great also in the entire self-effacement which marks his life. In the presence of Him Whom he came to announce, he shrank into glad obscurity. The herald's work was accomplished when the King arrived. And with untroubled heart he saw his own followers attach themselves to the One Whom he also followed. These are marks of true greatness in any servant of Christ.

But let us not be forgetful that such an one died ignominiously in a prison. For it is ever the world's recognition and reward of men whom the Lord terms great, to reject and despise them.

CHAPTER II

" *Let us now go even unto Bethlehem* " (*v.* 15).

IF the Gospel mirror be broken into a thousand fragments, each one still mirrors in itself the reflection of Christ. In this way the first Christmas Day is a miniature of His whole life, and a prophecy of all that should come to be the record of His redemptive work. To gather with the shepherds in the stable at Bethlehem, is to worship none other than the Lord of Life and Glory.

For here is the manifestation of everlasting love in the Father's gift, and in the Son's grace. Here is the Word made flesh. Prophecy has become power; language has assumed life; love has planned and love has stooped. This is the Evangel of the manger, which all His subsequent life unfolds; and it shines out against a background of gloom—the shadow of the world's rejection. For even the life of the helpless Babe is sought by a ruthless foe. The borrowed cradle foretells the borrowed tomb of the Man Who should one day die for the sins of His own rejectors. These are some of the lessons of the great Sacrifice learned by those who betake them to Bethlehem.

Here, too, is the worship and consecration of believing hearts. For here the rich and poor, the wise and unlearned, meet together in common fellowship. Already He draws all men to Him, and changes life for them. The rich pour out their treasures of gold, frankincense, and myrrh at His feet. The poor leave the yet greater treasure of their devotion, and go forth to proclaim Him in the testimony of captured hearts. Bethlehem becomes to them all the starting-point of a new life. From henceforth they are not their own.

How much do we need to urge one upon
another this Gospel of pilgrimage : " Let us
now go even unto Bethlehem." To us all it
means the pilgrimage of the sinful way. Along
the track of our own failures we must make
our way, through the wreckage of our own ideals
and vows, to the feet of the lowly Jesus; there
to find in Him both rest and renewal. From
thence alone do we go out to " walk in the light
even as He is in the light."

CHAPTER III

" *Thou art My beloved Son, in whom I am
well pleased* " (*v.* 22).

THE open Heaven, the descending Spirit, and
the approving Voice, all attest Christ as the Son
of God in the most solemn hour of His life, when
at His baptism He publicly assumed the place
of sinful man to fulfil all righteousness. Hitherto
He has been the Son of God disguised. Henceforth He is the Son of God manifested with
power, as the Saviour and Master of men.

The importance of the heavenly Voice is in
the light which it casts upon the previous silent
years of Christ's life. He had lived the quiet
uneventful life of a peasant-carpenter amid the
hills of Galilee, doing ordinary duties, and illuminating the village homestead with the light of

His gracious presence. He had entered into the common brotherhood of toil, making chairs and tables and ploughs, for wages. And He had tasted something of the poverty and restriction in which the lives of the greatest number of His people in all ages have been passed. He had lived, too, amid frankly unsympathetic relations, some of whom at least were incapable of appreciating His ideals, or of recognizing His claims. His was just an ordinary life, God-fearing and man-loving, with nothing of startling event or adventure to break its monotony.

And it was just in these commonplace circumstances that He had so lived as to secure the approval of the Heavenly Father. Every detail of life had been undertaken as in His sight, and every relationship sustained as in His will. Hence the Father's inspiring approbation as He set out on the pathway of the redemptive toil.

What an inspiration is this to those of us who have to live in narrow and cabined surroundings, bound to duties seemingly out of proportion to our spiritual endowments. The knowledge that these things in which our lot strangely resembles His in Nazareth, furnish us with all that is necessary for pleasing God, is a sanctifying inspiration. He is not hard to please, but we must give ourselves wholly to His service as did our Brother and Master.

CHAPTER IV

" To Nazareth, where He had been brought up " (*v.* 16).

THE pathway of spiritual blessing is always in the same direction. Every special season of fellowship with God, every new experience of His grace, and every fresh enduement of power, leads on to life in the sphere of the commonplace. Nazareth, to Christ and to His followers also, signifies the ordinary life with its demands and duties, its relationships and responsibilities, which none can rightly avoid. It is the most difficult sphere of all; for it is the place where we are best known, where our failures are least excused, and where our ideals not infrequently meet with little sympathy. But it is there that our witness is of greatest value, and that the results of faithfulness, though not always visible, are most certain.

Christ's return to Nazareth was obviously with the intent to make the Word of God intelligible to the people with whom He had companied during all the previous years. In the power of the Spirit He went back to those to whom He must always have been something of a mystery, to make His first declaration of

Messiahship, and to open to them the spiritual meaning and value of the Scriptures they already knew in the letter only. In His hand the old rod budded, and the familiar words were vitalized; until, ere long, the men of Nazareth were confronted with the plain issues which are always set before those to whom the Word of God comes in power.

In the same way life opens out into the service of the Kingdom for each one who like Him has realized the secrets of personal victory and sufficiency. Blessing to the people of Nazareth is the interpretation of the Divine appointment under which so many of His servants are compelled to abide there; even though, as in the case of the Lord Himself, that service may sometimes lead but to entire rejection. As He was, so are we responsible only for bringing men into contact with God. The rest is the work of His Sovereign Spirit.

CHAPTER V

" *New wine in old bottles* " (*v.* 38).

IN the double parable of new cloth on an old garment, and new wine in old bottles, Christ describes His own work as well as the character of the gifts with which He blesses those who come to Him. He came to clothe men with a new garment, and to satisfy them also with a new and abiding stimulation. And both garment and wine are unique and essential.

He imparts a new force of life which is like new wine with all its native qualities of expansion, fermentation, and disruption. Its form and action cannot be governed by precedent. The man who has come to know Christ must express his grateful love in original manner. Such an one will obey, and suffer, and labour to the uttermost; not because of any external imperative, but because of love's inner constraint. There is an imperiousness in the Divine life which cannot suffer the bondage of the ordinary order. New wine demands new bottles.

Under this figure Christ warns the individual and the Church alike against the possible double loss of both wine and vessels. For no tragedy is greater than that of hindered or ultimately lost enthusiasms, because they are seldom recoverable; just as new wine when spilled is seldom if ever gathered again. Herein is the peril of the man or the Church, who while desiring new life is yet unwilling for the necessary reconstruction of that in which it is to be contained and conserved. And this principle is of wide application in many directions. To understand it rightly removes the emphasis of life from things non-essential to things vital. For after all, the size and shape of the bottle is as nothing compared to the precious content ; and only as we recognize this can we minister to the world as the representatives of the Lord.

CHAPTER VI

" Why call ye Me, Lord, Lord, and do not the things that I say ? " (v. 46).

THERE is nothing of mere sentiment or theory about Christ's reign in the surrendered heart. It is an entirely practical matter, extending to every detail, and embracing every duty of our lives. For if we enthrone Him Lord by the consecration of ourselves, His will of necessity becomes the unquestioned law of our living. " Whatsoever He saith," solves for us every question, cuts the Gordian knot of every difficulty, and shows us the way out of every strait place. And in so recognizing Him in that which is His by right, all His power becomes available for life and service. This is the only sufficient dynamic for His people.

It is not enough to hold correct opinions regarding Him, nor to use correct phraseology about Him. It is not enough to wear His livery and to throng His courts. The one proof of reality is obedience. For if He is Lord He leaves men in no manner of doubt as to His requirements ; nor are His commandments grievous, albeit they set up the highest possible standard of life. And it is obedience to Him which differentiates His people from the world. Instead of the fashions and conventions by which the world is swayed, " the things that I say " are of supreme and unquestioned authority to them. As they go on with the Master, His servants soon cease to find favour with the multitude.

This life of reinforced obedience assures both a fulfilment of His purpose amongst men, and the discipline and preparation of His disciples for the eternal service which awaits them. For did He not say that entrance to the Heavenly Kingdom is denied to those who merely say " Lord, Lord," and awarded only to those who do the will of the Father as He has disclosed it ? Lip-service is of all forms of unreality the most deadly, and the most far-reaching in its influence. See to it then that we avoid it as the foe alike of our own souls and of His glory.

CHAPTER VII

" *Blessed is he, whosoever shall not be offended in Me* " (*v.* 23).

One of the commonest perils of the Christian life is that of being offended in Christ. The fellow-ship to which He calls us inevitably inspires a constant new and humiliating discovery of self, an unvarying disturbance of established order as

His will corrects our own, and a ceaseless effort to
attain, as followers, to the ideal which He, our
Forerunner, has set before us.   It is always peri-
lously possible, by reason of failure to obey and
to keep step with Him, by our lagging behind
or turning aside from the compelling guidances
of His companionship, to put ourselves unconsciously but actually far out of touch with
Him.

It is surely the most startling of all Christ's
warnings that men should find any possible
occasion of stumbling in Him.   We are prepared to find it in the world, in the opposition
of the devil, in the proven insincerity of others—
but in Him!   And yet experience assures us
that it is no remote nor impossible contingency.
For who does not know some disappointment of
hope, some failure of expectation, the weariness
of an unanswered prayer, or the ache of a crushed
heart which seems to evoke no sympathetic
answer from the Lord ?   And who does not know
how all this generates an unspoken and almost
unspeakable distrust, a feeling that we have not
been treated quite fairly, which develops in time
into actual resentment, until His yoke becomes
positively irksome, and we challenge His right
to control our lives ?   Sooner or later, if unchecked, this spirit ends in secret repudiation
of His lordship, and often in outward renunciation also of all spiritual hopes and aims.

From such small beginnings of distrust do
spiritual failures grow. To resist them sted-
fastly in faith is the life-conflict which is fraught
with the blessedness of the unoffended. All who
set themselves to it are enriched beyond words
with a sanctifying experience of self-victory,
and of deepened union with their Lord.

CHAPTER VIII

" That which he seemeth to have " (*v.* 18).

THERE is a law which governs the permanence
of all things in the moral and spiritual realms
of life, as indeed on other planes also. The real
alone is abiding, the unreal is only transient.
It is this law which the Saviour enforces when
He declares that the things which a man merely
seems to have shall inevitably be taken away
from him. He is not here declaiming against
positive hypocrisy, but is rather warning those
who are in danger of self-deception. He never
encourages morbid introspection, but there is
a time when self-examination is entirely necessary ; and it is to such honest self-inspection
that Christ summons His disciples with these
words. Reality is one of the key-notes of the
Gospel ; nor is it too much to say that He sets
greater store upon reality in His followers than
upon any other attitude of the heart.

Life is made up of occasions of test. There
come to all men tests of duty and crises of
spiritual need, in which the reality of faith, and
strength, and courage is tested. If these qualities
have hitherto been but an imagined possession,
or an adopted pose, the pressure of such crisis
hours will completely sweep them away. Like
the acid of the assayer, such experiences reveal
the quality of the metal, and unerringly detect
the true gold and the merely gilded.

It is certain, too, that a man's seeming possessions are taken from him when face to face
with death. For although death cannot take
anything from us which we really possess, it can
and does reveal what is unreal. When on the
threshold of the King's presence-chamber it is
difficult for any man to continue to deceive
himself. And if this is true of the portal, what
can be said of the judgment-seat? Reality
alone will endure the trial of the revealing fire,
and all "the wood, hay, and stubble" which
have been painted to represent "gold, silver, and
precious stones" will be condemned.

In the face of these things, how important it
is that we assure ourselves as to the reality of
our hold upon the things of abiding worth !

CHAPTER IX

"Ashamed of Me and of My words" (*v.* 26).

ONE of the prominent notes in the harmony
of Christ's teaching is that saving relationship
with Him is in the nature of the case visible.
A man's faith is not always necessarily articulate,
but if true it is always readily so. The most
pitiful of all sights is that of professed discipleship which is yet over-mastered by some false
shame. For of all things this is the greatest
deterrent of moral and spiritual progress. Its
cause is always difficult to analyse, for it is
commonly in such entire contradiction to other
qualities obviously possessed. How many there
are who are neither ignorant nor careless regarding Christ's claims, who are not without admiration of Him, who are by no means prayerless in
their own hours of need, and who nevertheless
fail to identify themselves with Him in a courageous and unmistakable allegiance. Their
inexplicable fear renders every other instinct
void. They are obviously under the power of
some consideration stronger than that of conscience and of Christ.

Christ never threatens men even when their
faults are those of moral cowardice—the most
inexcusable of all. But He does frankly reveal
the ultimate issue of such an attitude toward

Himself. Projected into eternity, which is the true test of every action, He declares the solemn fact that retribution is cast in the mould of its own sin. Our shame of Him will then be visited by His eternal shame of us. The Nemesis which overtakes the man who hides his face from Christ lest he should be shamed before the world, is unspeakable.

How blessed is the Evangel which declares Christ's power to deliver us both from blame before God and from shame before men ! The one who knows Him thus can but sing the triumph-song of faith and love : " I am not ashamed, for I am persuaded ! "

CHAPTER X

" Go and do thou likewise " (v. 37).

CHRIST's story of the Good Samaritan is appropriate to every age, illustrating as it does the kind of life which Christ commends and commands. It voices His condemnation of the elaborate religious profession which is divorced from human pity, and contrasts the relative values of creed and conduct, of doctrine and duty, in terms so vivid as to arrest the attention of all. It declares the true relation of faith and life, and emphasizes love to God in terms of love to man as being of supreme worth.

Under Christ's illumination, the conduct of

the Samaritan has become for all time the
pattern of the Christian life. For the opportunity
which he seized of ministering to one in need, is
always recurring in one form or another in a world
where men are constantly falling by the wayside.
Those who are self-absorbed are always unable
to recognize the voice of God in the cry of human
need. Such are a standing contradiction of their
own profession. Those whose lives are consecrated to Him Whom they love are inspired to
quick recognition and self-sacrifice service. And
such are in themselves a confirmation by which
the world is convinced of the reality of Christ.

Some service is only rendered under stress
of compulsion. Its voice is : " I must ; " and
invariably even its best deed lacks all that could
make it of value. Other service is rendered
under the constraint of duty. Its voice is :
" I ought." This is admittedly an advance ;
but by no means can the one who is thus spurred
ever realize either the joy or the effectiveness of
the true ministry. Then there is service of which
love alone is the impulse. Its voice is : " I may."
It regards obligation as privilege, and looks upon
every opportunity to serve as an honour. It gives
without stint, and places no restrictions upon its
sacrifices. And it is to this latter that Christ
commits His followers when He bids them
emulate the anonymous Samaritan. For He
Himself is the Model.

CHAPTER XI

"*A greater than Solomon is here*" (*v.* 31).

LOOKED at superficially, how unlikely does Christ's claim appear. For the contrast between Solomon's wealth and Christ's poverty, between his splendour and Christ's insignificance, between his kingship and Christ's homelessness, is almost staggering. And yet how completely justified is this declaration in the light of all that Christ has done and is!

He is greater than Solomon as a teacher, for His view of life is truer and worthier. Solomon certainly inculcates high ethical standards, but he records also the testimony of a disillusioned and disappointed man. For maxims do not make for morality, nor proverbs for purity. The man who evidenced such keen insight into the facts of life is the one whose last word records that "all is vanity." How different from this is the teaching of Christ! He both broadens the basis of sin and elevates the height of holiness, beyond anything that Solomon conceived. And yet He does not thereby cast men down to despair; for the theoretic perfection of His Word is always advanced along with its dynamic strength.

Christ is greater than Solomon also as a builder, for while Solomon's greatest achieve-

ment was the building of the Temple, Christ
builds living temples, each one of whom is as
a living stone in the eternal habitation of God.
From the quarry of sin He rescues men, shaping
and refining them by His Spirit, and thus making
them meet for the Divine indwelling. Living
temples of the Holy Ghost are the verification of
Christ's transcendent greatness. If Solomon could
evoke the admiration of Sheba's queen, how much
more should He inspire us to devoted and loyal
obedience !

CHAPTER XII

"*The very hairs of your head are all
numbered*" (*v. 7*).

THIS is an item of Christ's figurative teaching
which brings both comfort and uplift to His
people, declaring as it does the Divine ordering
of life's smallest trifles. Its importance is readily
recognized in the fact that life for most people
consists mainly of an aggregation of little things,
of which experience attests the power and
influence. Christ makes it abundantly plain
that bigness and greatness are not to be confused,
and thus interprets life to us all. The inference
of His statement is that in life's affairs size and
strength are sometimes strangely dispropor-
tionate. Indeed, the story of our greatest joys
and sorrows commonly has its beginning in

something which at the time seems entirely negligible. How good it is to know that God cares for the smallest things that concern His children, and invites them to seek His counsel and control about them all! For life's minutiae are love's ministry.

In this heartening declaration there is surely an injunction also that if God is careful for the small matters of our lives so, too, must we be. If we are His, the largest care must be devoted to the lowliest concern. And herein is the severest discipline of the soul. The small irritations of spirit, the unheralded opportunities of service, the hasty thoughtlessness of speech or action, and the unseen occasions of self-sacrifice which are in every life, demand constant vigilance and the exercise of sensitive obedience. For these are the trifles which go to make up that Christian character which is our strongest witness before the world, and His most powerful authentication.

CHAPTER XIII

" Journeying toward Jerusalem " (*v.* 22).

Christ's last journey from Galilee to Calvary is illustrative of His whole life. Prophecy had declared of Him that His face should be set as a flint, and so indeed it was. For with His

prevision of the Cross and His natural shrinking
from the Cup, there characterizes His life
a steady determination to do the Will of God
despite every dissuasion. His consecrated resolve,
with its disregard of all easy compromise, sets
Him forth for all time in the matchless beauty
of Divine love. For He saw not only the dark
thunder-cloud which hung over Jerusalem as He
directed His way thither, and which He knew
must break in storm upon Him. Beyond it, He
beheld also the light of the world's redemption.
Every mile of that journey proclaims His
inspiring consciousness of the worth of a sinful
soul.

As He journeyed, His disciples followed Him,
and this fact, too, is a parable of life. For He
is ever leading His people out into redemptive
service which can only be accomplished by their
entire self-sacrifice. To follow in His steps is to
cultivate the high determination of subordinating
everything to the fulfilment of the purpose to
which He inspires. As with Him, so with us
also, temptations to turn aside to an easier
pathway abound. But when faithfulness is most
difficult it is most necessary; for its issues are
immeasurable. All the strength of courage and
continuance which it demands are unfailingly
ministered to those who maintain unbroken
fellowship of purpose and aim with their Lord
and Leader.

CHAPTER XIV

" *Counteth the cost* " (*v.* 28).

CHRIST never disguises from men the cost of discipleship, in order to invest His Gospel with added attractiveness. He is content to call out the heroic latent in every man, and to base His appeal for faith and consecration, not on the ease, but on the difficulty and worthiness of life in the will of God. Thus it is that He deprecates rash and ill-considered profession, and urges that each one should first count the cost before identifying himself with Him. In His conception life is both a building and a battle. To set out upon it in either of these forms, without considering well the available resources for completion of the one and conquest in the other, is to court disaster.

How different in this Christ is from all other causes which seek the suffrages of men's lives ! Think, for instance, of the way in which sin disguises the cost. The last counsel it ever gives when offering its seductive delights is as to its own consequence. Its harvest is invariably hidden in the delights of the seed-sowing ; and hence it is that men give themselves over to unworthiness with never a thought of a day of reckoning. Christ seeks deliberate and calculated loyalty as the only guarantee of future

steadfastness. He declares that the cost of
fellowship with Himself is nothing less than
a complete renunciation of sin, an entire surrender of self, and an open declaration of faith
before the world. Those who are prepared for
this are gladly welcomed to His company, and
appointed to His service. And all the history of
His Church records the fact that it is those who
do first count this cost and then cast in their lot
with Him, who subsequently exhibit magnificent
recklessness in the carrying out of His will.
To them no opposition comes as a surprise,
and no personal affront is a deterrent. For it
is with full consciousness of such that they
enlist.

CHAPTER XV

"This man receiveth sinners" (*v.* 2).

THE testimony of Christ's enemies, if col-
lected, would almost afford us a complete
Gospel. Indeed, had we no other record of His
life than of those things which His opponents
said about Him, we should still know enough of
His character, His message, His power, and His
love, to draw out our hearts toward Him in
trust and obedience. This taunting sneer of the
Pharisees has long since become the boast of His
people. The fact that " He receiveth sinners

and eateth with them " is His supreme attractiveness and assurance to those who are conscious of their own greatest need.

Part of the sweet harmony of the Gospel is
that while Christ came with a mission for all,
He came also with a message to each. He did
not deal with evil in the mass but in the man.
He did not attack the problem of sin, so much
as the problem of the sinner; and of these He
never despaired of the worst. The natural order
in the world of men and events proclaims the
survival of the fittest as the law of life. In complete contradiction, Christ puts the salvation
of the unfittest in the forefront of His programme.

He receives sinners into fellowship by first of
all creating in them a moral and spiritual
correspondence with Himself. For there is
nothing in any man whose sin is yet upon him
which qualifies him for such holy companionship. The miracle of the new birth must recreate
deteriorated capacities, repair devastated moral
powers, and inspire new aims before the Saviour
and the sinner actually become one. And of this
miracle He alone is the doer in the life of " whosoever will."

CHAPTER XVI

" Ye cannot serve God and mammon " (v. 13).

OF all Christ's sayings this is perhaps the one
to which men in all ages have paid the least
heed. He emphatically declares that in order
to serve and please God a man must be volun-
tarily free from the strong bondage of material
things. The conflicting claims of God and of
earthly riches must be settled at the very
beginning. In Himself Christ exemplified this
principle, and for all time set us an example
of utter independence of the world, amounting
indeed to positive scorn of its spurious treasures;
while at the same time devoting Himself to its
highest and eternal interests. In this as in all
things else, it is enough for the servant that he
be as his Lord.

Nothing is more evident than the fact that
men—even men of professed faith—do become
ensnared and enslaved by mammon. Almost
all the struggles of life have as their object its
acquisition or its retention. And of all things
certain in our common life, nothing is more so
than the fact that those who serve mammon
must do it with all their heart, and soul, and
mind, and strength. It is not hard to recognize also that such become its bond-slaves.
For earthly treasure is above all things tyran-

nical. The grip of gold upon men's hearts is unrelenting.

This is the reason for Christ's drastic pro-hibition. Mammon demands the place which can only rightly be given to God. Its claims are so entirely at variance with the call of the highest as to render it entirely impossible for any man to make a success in both realms. What we most desire and most earnestly strive after is either our assurance of sonship or our condemnation.

CHAPTER XVII

" Remember Lot's wife " (*v.* 32).

CHRIST'S emphatic reminder of the peril of unreality is like a buoy placed over a dangerous reef, for the warning of unwary navigators. The story is one of sin and its unimagined conse-quence, of grace and its unappreciated gifts, of love and its unavailing efforts. Despite all that Divine power did to secure her salvation, Lot's wife is for ever a warning example of unbelief. Out of heart-agreement with God's proclaimed wrath on Sodom's sin, and with but slight regard for His proffered mercy, her heart was really in the city along with her imperilled possessions. With her, looking back really meant a lingering

of desire ; and her punishment is but an illustration of the sudden and unexpected withdrawal of
opportunity which comes upon some, and of the
hardening of heart and conscience which comes
upon all in similar case.

This injunction to "remember Lot's wife" is
directed toward those who like her would save
more than themselves. It warns those who are
trying to make the best of both worlds, but who
in the attempt fail to keep step with the Angel-
messengers of God. It declares the destructive
power of a look, in which there lurks evidence
of a lustful mind and an unbelieving heart. The
awful possibility of being almost saved and yet
entirely lost, is one about which Christ leaves no
man in uncertainty. It is safer to toy with
forked lightning than to trifle with the revealed
Will of God. For none can play fast and loose
with the tremendous facts of sin, and judgement,
and grace, without jeopardizing thereby their
own souls. In the midst of all the world's
already-condemned seductiveness, let us lay
to heart this startling warning. To have the
peril of unbelief is to have also the fear of God
before our eyes.

CHAPTER XVIII

" God be merciful to me a sinner " (*v.* 13).

THE startling contrast between the prayers of the Pharisee and the publican furnishes an indication of Christ's standards of value, as applied to the most important realm of men's lives—their approach to God. For some men God can do nothing. Their attitude of heart toward Him, their self-sufficiency and self-complacency, ward off the beneficent intentions of His grace. Their bodies may posture in His house, but their spirits are an immeasurable distance from Him ; and the only result of their miscalled worship is in the continued hardening and deadening of their moral sense. As in Nature the action of some streams tends to turn living objects into stone, so does the stream of unfelt and mechanical and self-seeking praying petrify the soul of its offerer.

How simple as to form and direct as to request is the prayer of the publican. Standing " afar off " in the consciousness of the sin which separated him from God, he realized that he was yet alone with Him. " God . . . mercy . . . me " are the notes of his heart's cry. But he has already come to know that the span of mercy bridges the sin-gulf, and is confident that even such an one as he is may safely venture across. On

its further side the Father awaits him with
a welcome which is unmixed with any reproach.
Over that scene a veil is drawn, and the sacred
intimacy is unrecorded. But from its strengthening assurance the man goes down to his house to
declare what God has done for him. He has
learned by an experience which nothing can
modify, that sin confessed is sin covered, and
that life humbled is life exalted. And this is
sufficient inspiration for the long moral conflict
that is yet before him. Such prayer is the one
gateway to the life victorious and beautiful,
alike for him and for us. It demands our stoop-
ing, but it ensures our salvation.

CHAPTER XIX

" To-day I must abide at thy house " (*v.* 5).

For one day only did Christ visit Jericho as
He pursued His way toward Calvary. His
coming thither, however, and all that He did
there is a perfect picture of His entire redeeming
purpose and work. A single dew-drop may
mirror a star as clearly as does an ocean ; and
any one of Christ's days reveals the grace of God
as truly as does His whole life. For He is ever
the Son of Man seeking the lost, and compassing
their salvation by every means of which He is
Master.

How entirely does His Evangel transcend any
man's highest desires! Zacchaeus would have
been well content to catch a passing glimpse of
Him. His curiosity would have met its full
reward had he but seen Him. He is all unconscious that behind his immediate thought Christ
had already detected something deeper and
worthier. And he does not know that He has
come to Jericho for the express purpose of
blessing him. There are two searchers each
looking for the other when any man begins to
seek Christ.

To what heights does Christ lift those who
are responsive to His call, and who make their
decision to obey Him without fear before all
beholders! For He identifies Himself with them,
and at once shares the responsibilities to which
in that hour they pledge themselves. Having
come into the heart, He proceeds to come into
the home, where His presence soon reveals all
that is out of harmony with the requirements
of Divine holiness. And with this creation of
self-consciousness comes the realization of His
abundant assistance. Such a partnership of
power alone secures the costly cleansing of any
life from its moral discrepancies. The indwelling
Christ Himself makes the heart meet for His
own habitation. Best of all He accepts the poor
hospitality of men that are sinners. And they
sit at the table with Him.

CHAPTER XX

" *Render unto God the things that be God's* " (*v.* 25).

CHRIST'S answer to the carping critics who ever sought to entangle Him in His talk, has for all time lifted every matter of personal interest and responsibility into direct relationship with the Will of God. The truth of the Divine Fatherhood which is the centre of His message, implies that men belong wholly to God ; and that therefore it is incumbent upon every one to yield to Him all that with which life is endued and entrusted.

Every capacity of the soul is stamped with God's image and superscription. As the name upon a coin denotes its nominal possession by the sovereign, so the stamp of God's creation and ownership is upon every human power and aptitude. Sin may dim, but it can never wholly deface this attestation of God's crown-right. Thus it is that no man can be entirely true to himself who withholds from God's use any part of his life.

Such a relationship with God as Christ enjoins is never entered upon in any mere haphazard way. No man ever drifts thoughtlessly into positive and practical surrender of himself to the Divine claim and control. To render unto God

the things which are His involves a very definite
and considered action on the part of every one
of us.   That action develops into an attitude
which must be daily and hourly maintained, in
which the yielded soul gladly and practically
acknowledges that he is not his own but is
" bought with a price," and is hence eternally
involved in the responsibility of glorifying God in
body and spirit.   Life on any lower plane fails of
its purpose.   This, indeed, is the tragedy of many
an enlightened one, that consecration does not
wait upon conviction, and that loyalty of heart is
not the outcome of light from heaven.   Such ones
may rise to great height, in the court of Caesar,
while in the Kingdom of God they simply have no
existence.

CHAPTER XXI

" Take heed to yourselves " (v. 34).

No one understands the strange insincerities
of the human heart as Christ does.   The mysterious conflict between ideals and tendencies,
and the perplexing contrast between intentions
and instabilities, as they exist even in His most
ardent followers, are all well known to Him.
He never discourages the warm impulses of
affection, nor despises the courage which would
do and dare for Him.   He does, however, frankly
endeavour to create a consciousness of personal

insufficiency which will at all times drive His people to Himself. For in Him alone there is grace both to cover their sins and to strengthen and stablish their lives. Nothing can be effectively substituted for this; not even the splendour of a great hope as bright as is that of His return.

Indeed it is in view of the certainty of His coming again, and of the uncertainty also which invests that day, that He bids us exercise watchful vigilance over ourselves. It almost seems incongruous in such a connexion to speak as He does of eating and drinking as amongst the causes liable to involve men in the condemnation of unreadiness. And yet it is just the things of the body which most often dull the sensibilities of the soul. Even the hearts of Christian men may become so overcharged with these things as to render them prisoners of their own lower nature. For God does not shift from any man the responsibility of choice and of will. There are details of life the ordering of which He leaves entirely to the loyalty of His servants, though never without giving them clear and ample direction as to their own good and His own glory. How earnestly should we regard these words of Christ, questioning ourselves as to the supreme dominance under which we live. Are the things of the body uppermost, or the things of the Spirit? Are we walking after the desires of the flesh, or after the mind of God? Are we

devoted to the pleasures of sin, or to the service
of our Lord ? The answer which conscience
unerringly gives to the one who thus sincerely
questions with himself, is the truest confidence
of his readiness for the return of the King.

CHAPTER XXII

" *I have prayed for thee* " (*v.* 32).

WHAT interpreting light does Christ cast upon
the sore mystery of our common temptations. It is
only when viewed in the light of His Evangel that
we see them as being allowed in order to equip
us for the service of strengthening others. They
are not prevented by Divine love just because
they are entirely necessary to our truest life.
The permissive Will of God is disclosed behind
the malignant purpose of the Adversary. He
would sift us with the purpose of destroying the
wheat and saving the chaff. God allows temptation to reach His children with the introverted
purpose of destroying the chaff and saving the
wheat. All that belongs to the old life, i.e. the
chaff which is round about the true grain, must
be got rid of. The tempers, habits, and dis-
positions which are no part of the new life, we
can only lose by the sifting which God permits.
The process is at once painful and perplexing ;
and there is real danger lest faith fails under it.

What an inspiration to the tempted and mystified believer is Christ's assurance of prayer on his personal behalf !

Christ's supplication for His tempted people is not to be understood as a repetition of request, but as the unceasing presentation of His propitiation. In His Sacrifice once offered He has fulfilled the condition by which God's grace henceforth flows to men, through Himself as the channel. And at the Throne of Grace, He ever pleads the merit of His blood on behalf of His beloved.

It is as though Christ looks upon every life as a grain of wheat in view of its potential harvest. His concern is that nothing of this should be lost; and His intercession is a silent partnership of power to this end. For beyond the experience of victory and development, which is the ideal outcome of temptation, there lies a ministry of strength-giving to other tempted and suffering lives. This is only possible to the man who has himself suffered, and has come through with strengthened faith and firmer hold upon God. Experience alone is equipment in spiritual service. It is that the man of God may be " thoroughly furnished unto all good work " that Christ unceasingly prays for us. Let us therefore endeavour to establish others in this consciousness, and ever bind to ourselves this strengthening word : " I have prayed for thee."

CHAPTER XXIII

" He answered him nothing " (*v.* 9).

No recorded tragedy is greater than the silence of Christ toward the man who questioned Him in the supreme hour of His life. How strangely different it is to His ready conversation with men of all kinds and classes as He companied with them. No leper so loathsome, no fallen woman so vile, no outcast so sunken, but Christ speaks to them the Wonderful Words of Life. Here, however, on the throne is one to whom Christ will not condescend, and whose entire condemnation is in the thing which Christ refused to say. For Herod's mind had by this time become utterly reprobate. He who knew to do right had deliberately done it not, and hence his sin remained. Slowly but surely deterioration of character and atrophy of moral nature had set in; until, when at last Christ is before him he is unable to recognize anything in Him but a mere wonder-worker, whose reputed skill might while away a tedious hour. His questions to the Lord reveal his lost capacity for holiness, and the entire vitiation of all his springs of thought. To such a man Christ has nothing to say. Deaf ears make a dumb Christ. He will not speak to him because there is nothing to appeal to.

But let it be noted that Christ's silence is

not merely because Herod had sinned, else
would He be silent to every one of us as we cry
to Him.   One word of real confession and
repentance had secured for even Herod the
fullness of His pardoning mercy.   But he is
joined to his idols and Christ lets him alone.
He will not cast His pearls before swine nor give
that which is holy unto dogs ; and by continued
persistence in sin despite God and conscience
Herod has become a mere animal.   What
warning is this strange silence of the Son of
God to us all.   Well may we pray with the
Psalmist " be not silent to me oh Lord, lest
I become like unto them that go down to
the pit."

CHAPTER XXIV

" *Peace be unto you* " (*v.* 36).

PEACE is the inspiring salutation of the One
who has made peace by the Blood of His Cross.
It is the first word of His risen life, and the
last word of His departing benediction.   For
all time it expresses the paradox of the Christian
life, which though passed amid endless agitation
and committed to ceaseless conflict, is yet itself
unruffled and untroubled.   The peace which
Christ bequeaths is that which was seen in His
own life.   Its blessedness is the result not of
the absence of loss or sorrow, but of the un-

changing presence of God. Hence it can sustain
any test and be known in any circumstances.
It is the Heavenly heartsease whose perfume
unmistakably clings to the followers of Christ
amid the fuss and bustle of the unresting throngs
of the world's life.

As with the disciples in the upper room with
its locked doors, so too with us, peace may
be lost by doubt, or fear, or preoccupation.
Already in the days that have gone, Christ had
spoken peace to their hearts; but now their
assurance of its power had gone from them.
The startling events of that memorable week
when all the waves and billows of sorrow had
gone over them had wellnigh driven them from
their foundation. Nervous apprehension of
certain opposition in the immediate future had
undone them. In such a case the mere mention
of peace seems a mockery, were it not Jesus
Himself Who appeared speaking the old sweet
greeting instinct as ever with strengthening
promise, to assure them that events cannot
affect facts. For He, too, had suffered far more
than they, far more indeed than any of the sons
of men since the world began. And He is still
able to give to others the peace which He Himself had never lost. His is the peace of the
triumphant Victor; and He bestows it as part
of the enduement of those who are to go forth
in His name to the conflict.

St. JOHN

CHAPTER I

" The Word was made flesh " (v. 14).

PRIOR to Christ's coming the Word of God
had already become human speech and writing.
In the main, however, men would not listen to
it, could not understand it, and did not interpret
it ; for, as a matter of fact, God cannot be
adequately declared in mere utterance and
literature. Hence the Word became flesh ; and
expressed God in all His human experiences,
not by teaching a doctrine, but by living a life
under ordinary human conditions of pain, disappointment, temptation, and joy. Only thus as
He reveals Him can the Infinite become intimate
to us, the Creator become the companion, and
the thunder of law form the deep diapason of
the tender harmonies of love.

In the Incarnation of Christ there is declared
the possibility of fellowship between man and
God, the restoration of sin-forfeited union.
That " the Word became flesh, and dwelt among
us," proclaims the glorious truth that God's
thoughts can come into men's minds, that His
works can be done by men's hands, and that
His affection can be responded to and reflected
in men's hearts. The Word living in human

flesh declares that not only are there contrasts
between man and God, but affinities also.

His appearance as a man amongst men is not
merely a truth to be believed, but a type also
of the life of which He is the Bestower and the
Forerunner. For in His followers language must
become life, and creed must become character.
It is only by such incarnation that the truth of
God secures its triumph in the world. The
Gospel is not commended by its Evangelical
tenderness, its historical accuracy, its scientific
consistency, or its ethical perfection, though it
has all of these, but by the Word becoming
flesh in us as in Him. The process of the
Christian life is to materialize the spiritual.
Under its discipline each man of faith becomes
the expression of some thought of God to the
world. Such honour have all His saints.

CHAPTER II

" Thou hast kept the good wine until now "
(*v.* 10).

THE story of the village wedding in Cana is
a significant illustration of Christ's work among
men. His presence, and that of His disciples,
doubtless strained the resources of the household,
and went far to explain the sudden shortage of
wine. And is it not always so, that where Christ

comes there is at first a disconcerting sense of insufficiency and need? Old delights, pursuits, and friendships seem strangely to lose their charm, and the disturbed heart cries out "What lack I?" Happy indeed is the one who, in that hour of self-discovery, when the wine of life runs short, turns to the Christ of Cana. For He ever makes this consciousness of need the opportunity of showing His power and glory.

The governor at that feast marvelled that the best vintage had been kept until the end of the festivities. In speaking, however, as he did he was all unconsciously enunciating the principle that seems to govern all Christ's gifts. For He is unlike every other in this respect, that He always gives the best last. For instance, sin always offers the best wine first and the worst last. First the brightness and pleasure, the good fellowship and self-gratification; but afterward the bitter consequence, the relentless memory, and the unending remorse. All the world's pleasures, too, are keenest at the beginning. The one who gives himself to its ideals finds that his very enjoyment and satisfaction rob him of zest, and destroy his power of desire. But Christ gives "not as the world giveth." It is always His way to lead on from grace to grace, from strength to strength, from glory to glory. With Christ to-morrow is always

better than to-day.   We journey with Him
not toward the night but toward the light.   The
more we know of Him, the fuller is our apprecia·
tion of all that He is and does.

And when the river is past and we gather with
Him in the Homeland, it will be to find that our
richest earthly joy in His love is entirely out·
distanced by the delight of His unveiled presence.
We shall find that He has kept the best wine
of all until then.

CHAPTER III

" He that doeth truth cometh to the light "
(*v.* 21).

THIS is Christ's comprehensive description of
the one who in union with Him sets out to live
the true life.   He describes him as one who
" doeth ", and not one who merely believeth the
truth.   By co-operation of faith and obedience
with the Divine purpose, he is ever striving to
make his life an approximation to Christ's ideal,
in a world where error rules and darkness holds
sway.   And the constant conflict thus involved
demands high communion and a sure confidence.

The translation of his own desires into actual
deeds of goodness is no easy thing for any man.
For not only is the opposition of the world
a deterring factor, but in himself he also finds

much to conflict with his purpose. His tendencies
are often in contrast to his aims; and his moral
weakness frequently mars his high endeavours.
Sometimes, too, the holy Vision fades in the
dazzling light in which sin presents itself, and
only a constant ministry of grace can then
enable him to continue in the Truth. But this
is secured to him by his determined coming to
the light. Daily he must bring his life into the
brightness of the sanctuary, submitting himself
to the scrutiny of the eyes of Divine love, which
are as a flame of fire. Searching and painful
though this revelation of self may be, it is the
only guarantee of steadfastness. For the light
which reveals sin shines also upon its remedy.
It can disclose nothing but what the Blood can
remove.

From the light it is evident that Christ intends
His people to go out into the darkness, and so
to live there as to declare unmistakably the
dynamic by which alone the life of discipleship
is possible. There is no mystery about the one
who *does* the Truth. It is manifest to all that
" his deeds are wrought in God." Thus is each
one an irrefutable witness to the reality of His
power.

CHAPTER IV

" I have meat to eat that ye know not of "
(v. 32).

THE surprise of the disciples on their return
to Jacob's Well is easy to understand. An hour
before they had left Christ wearied and hungry.
Now they find him refreshed and gladdened, and
without need of the food they had been at pains
to purchase. It was only afterward that they
learned the inwardness of His declaration as to
the resources of sustenance and strength of
which they knew not. In doing the will of the
Father in respect of a single sinful soul, He had
been renewed. And herein He seeks to train
His disciples in the same method of life, by
imparting the secret of His strength. There is
an interaction of spiritual strength and service
which means that enduement is actually increased by expenditure, when the direction of
the effort is the will of God. His is the Gospel
of action both in exhortation and example.
Work is really the staff of life ; and the man who
is busiest in the things of the Kingdom cannot
fail to be the strongest in his own faith and
assurance. It is service for God and souls
which alone makes the servant strong in patient
endurance and knowledge.
We are apt sometimes to imagine that the

task to which the will of God commits us is
beyond our powers. As a matter of fact,
strength is acquired, not in view of each task,
but as a result of doing it. Faithfulness in
that which is least, conditions force for that
which is greatest. How clearly do we see all
this in the life of the Lord Himself. He came
forth, not to speak of, not to trifle with, and
not to be resigned to the will of God, but to *do*
it. In all its variety, His life was always lived
in one direction—that of the blessing of souls.
Each accomplishment in this respect, brought
to Him a new acquisition of strength for further
service of the same sort. Only in the same
banqueting-house of active obedience can His
disciples likewise eat of the Hidden Manna.

CHAPTER V

*" How can ye believe which receive honour
one of another ? "* (*v.* 44).

How startling is Christ's discernment of
unbelief, significantly addressed to those whose
reputation was for searching the Scriptures.
The erection of a false standard—" honour one
of another," and the evasion of a first responsibility—" seek not the honour which cometh
from God only," makes them virtual unbelievers,
despite their religious observance or zeal for

the outward things of worship. Faith, in
Christ's meaning—which is the only one that
matters—always connotes obedience, which is
compact of the assent of the mind to a Truth,
the consent of the will to a Programme, and the
devotion of the heart to a Person. He conceives
the man of faith as first apprehending the Will
of God; then proceeding onward, in obedience,
with no concern as to the dissent or criticism
of others; and then finding along that pathway
self-discipline, brotherhood, service, and the
honour which God alone bestows—that of being
His representative and messenger to other men.

In challenging as to "how can you believe?"
Christ is in no sense declaiming against the
grateful courtesies of life, but is warning men
against making the world's favour the objective
of their life-aim. The peril of so ordering life
as to ensure being well spoken of and to avoid
adverse verdicts is a subtle and dangerous one.
For that sort of thing grows, until men come to
love the praise of other men more than the
praise of God. It becomes the strongest incen-
tive and influence of conduct. Under its sway,
self-knowledge is completely lost as a moral
factor of life; until ultimately capacity for faith
is injured beyond repair. On the other hand,
to love God and to seek after His honour
liberates men by its own force from all worldly
love and concern. This is the true independence

and glorious liberty of the children of God.
His unquestioned lordship and leadership alone
justifies our professions of faith.

CHAPTER VI

" I am the Bread of Life " (*v.* 35).

How surprising at first sight is Christ's
declaration, with its assumption of universal
hunger. He takes it for granted that all men
are hungry, and on this postulate announces
Himself as the One who is able to meet their
needs. He is constantly seeking to interpret
the longings of human souls, which are explicable
only in the light of His loving interest.

Hunger is a recurring manifestation of physical
health which we all recognize. So also is it in
the moral and spiritual realm. Hunger for the
highest and truest life is itself a sign of saving
relationship with God. This was the first
consciousness of the prodigal, who, " when he
came to himself," knew himself to be hungry
for love and for home. And it is this sense,
common to us all, which Christ endeavours to
explain and to direct towards Himself. For
He is the Divine provision for every hungry
soul. He says in effect : " Just as you cannot
live without bread, so you cannot truly live
without Me." And there is no greater mistake
than that of despising the commonplace, of

leaving the Bread and of turning to the daintier food of the world's tables which excites an appetite it can never satisfy. For if He is indeed the Bread of Life, to miss Him is to perish.

Under this figure of bread, He impresses upon us the necessity of personal appropriation, if we are to derive from Him any benefit of life or strength. For as uneaten bread is perfectly useless to strengthen, so an unappropriated Christ is powerless to save. Just also as we need to eat bread day by day, so is a daily taking of the Saviour's fullness needed, if we are to be strengthened by Him for the labours of life. Yesterday's food only serves to make that of to-day necessary. In spiritual as in material things, we can only live a day at a time.

CHAPTER VII

" If any man will do His Will, he shall know of the doctrine " (*v.* 17).

This of all Christ's proclamations is the one which resolves the difficulty of every honest and sincere seeker. It declares that God reveals Himself to individuals according to their attitude of will, and boldly submits every perplexity to a present and practical test which is available to every man. In effect, Christ says to those who profess a desire to know God : " Do as

much as you know, and you shall come to know
as much as you desire ! Walk in the beam before
you, and you shall come to the brightness which
is beyond you ! According to your sympathetic
determinations shall be your spiritual dis-
coveries ! " The order of the pilgrim's progress
is ever by way of instinct, will, and obedience,
to faith and knowledge. For men know of God
just what their own conduct justifies—and no
more.

Desires after God may co-exist with much
perplexity concerning Him. For men's quest
often gives birth to deep questionings, and their
vague prayer is not infrequently mixed with still
vaguer uncertainty. Such uncertainty may be
variously caused, by the seeming overthrow, for
instance, of things which hitherto have been
taken for granted, or by the impact of new
knowledge on old faith, or by the difficulty of
reconciling human experiences with Divine
assurances. But, however caused, Christ challenges a man's personal sincerity and consistency as the condition of all spiritual knowledge.
He declares that in the last analysis everything
depends on the attitude of his will. If one
honestly desires to do the will of God, and sets
himself resolutely to do it ; if he responds to
such knowledge as he already possesses, however
imperfect it is, and leaves matters not vital in
abeyance, Christ declares of him that he shall

come to the full knowledge of God which is life
eternal. This is the test which each of us must
apply to our individual lives. It is unerring
both in its judgement and its outcome.

CHAPTER VIII

" Neither do I condemn thee " (*v.* 11).

IN entire contrast to her treatment by the
Scribes and Pharisees is that meted out by
Christ to the sinful woman. Official religion can
only accuse and convict. Divine love makes the
fullest allowance for every contributing circum-
stance, and seeks rather the restoration of the
sinner than the punishment of her fault. It
matters not what are the forces which bring
such an one to His feet, nor how entirely is
direct punishment merited. Christ has not come
to condemn, but to save; and in speaking pardon
and peace to the crushed and broken soul He
is essentially true to Himself and to His mission.
With what assurance does His faithfulness in
this respect encourage every sin-stricken heart.
That He cares as much as He does, at once
invests the sin with awfulness, but inspires the
sinner with hope.

His attitude towards the accusers is as
significant as that towards the accused. Con-
temptuously silent at first at their effrontery in

covering their own sin while dragging into the light that of the erring woman, He subsequently challenges them with their own guilt, to their utter discomfiture. Conscience is always His ally in moral issues, and joins with Him in judgment upon all artificial distinctions. Sin covered and unconfessed always drives men from His presence in confusion.

In His pardon of the sinner, and His refusal to join in her condemnation, Christ reveals the gladdening fact that the ground of judgment for every man is not the sin he has committed, but rather the rejection of Himself—its Divine Remedy. It is on this account that He still utters these gracious words to every stained and contrite one. For the time of condemnation is not yet at hand, nor will be until the opportunity of accepting His pardon has for ever passed away.

CHAPTER IX

" One thing I know " (*v.* 25).

EXPERIENCE is indubitable. Mere opinions and theories are frequently quite unable to withstand the force of argument and the pressure of opposition. What a man has seen, however, with his own eyes he can never unsee. Though he may fail to convince those who con-

trovert him, his own assurance but deepens
with every fresh declaration of that which he
knows. Such is the case of the blind man, the
story of whose healing strikes such a tender and
human note in the Gospel record. Faith in
Christ and implicit obedience to His command
have been the means whereby the miracle has
been effected. The man hitherto imprisoned in
darkness is liberated in light entirely by the
power of the Son of God. That such an event
calls attention to Christ, and evokes a hostile
demonstration by His foes, is scarcely a cause of
wonder ; for it is ever so. That it is unable to
shake the confidence of the one who is enjoying
the glad amaze of a newly-discovered world, is
likewise not to be wondered at. Such an experience is entirely beyond the reach of all
question.

Ultimate and final certainty with regard to
Christ has to be sought by each man in the
realm of his own life. Where argument fails and
logic is insufficient, the victory is ever with the
one who can say : " I know ! " Ignorant concerning many things he may be, and fragmentary
even with regard to Christ may be his knowledge.
But the irrefutable proof of His reality and power
is in the realm of his own being. There the
unspeakable change has been wrought, and of
this " one thing " at least he is confident. He
may know but in part—yet he knows ! His

faith stands not in the wisdom of men but in
the power of God; and its declaration is a verit-
able Gospel to those who hear it. For this,
indeed, is the knowledge which is power.

CHAPTER X

*" I lay down My life that I might take it
again " (v. 17).*

In these words Christ enunciated a principle
which in His life and by His death He expanded
and illustrated. It is the law of His own being,
and that also of His followers, that " it is more
blessed to give than receive." There is in the
Gospel harmony the plaintive note of redeeming
sorrow; but there is also the deep undertone
of victorious fulfilment because of voluntary
sacrifice.

Christ's death was in no sense a mere object-
lesson of the love of God without propitiatory
significance. Still less was it the inevitable end
of a life lived out of touch with the current ideas
of the day, and hence but an example of moral
heroism. There is something in His simple
statement, " I lay down My life," which for
ever makes it impossible to doubt the volun-
tariness with which He undertook and carried
out the task of the world's redemption. As

a mere pulpit, the Cross is gruesome. As an altar, it is entirely glorious.

"The joy which was set before Him," was the anticipated delight of calling forth by His very sacrifice, such responsive love as should secure for Him undisputed sway over the lives of His loved ones. He laid His life down, that He might take it again in other souls. Wherever a sinful heart recognizes Him as Saviour, and gladly receives Him as Sovereign, there He sees of the travail of His soul. And all that may be said in this respect with regard to Him is true also with regard to His followers. Every Christian is in some sense a reincarnation of His Spirit. Sacrifice as the crown of life is a complete contradiction of the popular ideal, but it is the law of all true discipleship. For it is only by laying it down, that life's expansion is assured and its harvest made certain.

CHAPTER XI

"*Even now*" (*v.* 22).

THERE is perhaps no record of faith more significant and complete than is this word. Martha, at the tomb of her brother, full of a grief which was the keener because of the anticipated deliverance which had not come in time, when at last face to face with the Saviour,

was able from her broken heart to speak this
word of triumphant trust. "Even now" on
her lips voices the faith by which the dead was
ultimately raised. The difficulties of the present
are always those which we feel most keenly.
We cannot get away from the tyranny of
insistent fact, and it is often harder to believe
that God is with us now than to recognize His
past mercy, or to hope for His future blessing.
The problems and ills of the present seen at
close range appear greater than anything we
have ever known. Nor does the fact that these
are often part of the harvest of the past make it
any easier to regard them with equanimity.
Indeed, this consciousness renders it the more
difficult to realize that "even now" amid the
sin-created tangles of life, God is with us to
guide, strengthen, and to bless.

God's delays are never denials; and the one
who honestly seeks audience with Him, when
all is blackest and darkest, always finds power
to deliver and to relieve. "Even now," when
weakness is most felt, when opposition is most
fierce, when temptation is most severe, when
enthusiasm is most difficult to arouse, and when
need is most pressing—the presence of the living
Lord means light, and life, and liberty.

CHAPTER XII

" Not for Jesus's sake only, but that they might see Lazarus also " (*v.* 9).

MEN raised from the dead are themselves the media for the revelation of God's glory. People who carelessly pass by the offers and claims of the Saviour, are always arrested at the sight of one in whom so obviously His power is illustrated. Christ was no stranger to the crowd which gathered at Bethany. Doubtless they had all seen and heard Him in previous days. But the spectacle of a man raised from the dead, evoked all their curiosity and wonder, and filled them with something of the awe of the unseen world. With Christ's doctrine and teaching they might be at variance—honestly or dishonestly. But such a manifestation of His power they could neither disregard nor explain away. And so it ever is.

It is in redeemed men that the power of God unto salvation is exhibited to the world. " Ye are my witnesses " is Christ's abiding commission to those whom He has touched into life, and from whom the grave-clothes of sin have been unbound. Each one is an authentication of Him, stating the case for Him beyond all power of contradiction. With what a steadying responsibility does this fact invest our lives!

Many who will not hearken directly to Him
cannot fail to be arrested if we exhibit before
them the evidences of a new life. What a record
alike of Lazarus and ourselves is that which
declares that " by reason of Him many went
away and believed on Jesus " ! And what
a responsibility do we incur should the record
of our lives be the reverse of this !

CHAPTER XIII

" Now is the Son of man glorified " (*v.* 31).

Strange it is that as the end drew near, and
the shadows of the Garden and the Cross were
thrown darkly across His path, that Christ
should declare this to be the hour of His glory.
The circumstances are significant and illuminating. The traitorous follower had just gone out
into the night, after having received the sop—
the Master's last attempt to pierce his soul
with the arrow of unchanged love. The little
company was then truly of one heart in their
devotion to Him, the gold no longer mixed
with dross, nor the interest of the disciples
vitiated by any thing of disloyalty. This, then,
is the condition of Christ's glory. When all
that is unloving, self-seeking, and faithlessness
is cast out either of a community or a life—then
only is He glorified in His professed friends.

In how many hearts is the Judas spirit pre-
dominant ! Desire to gain material things is apt
to blind men as to the price which must be paid
for them. Fascination of the thing sought too
often hides the unworthiness of the means
adopted for its acquisition. Many an one only
acquires his wealth by betraying as Judas did
the Saviour whose name he bears. The spirit
of the world is at all times utterly opposed to
the spirit of Christ ; and it is impossible for
any to respond to a double dominance. If we
would glorify Him Who bought us with His
Blood for this very purpose, we must dethrone
every idol and cast out every usurper from the
kingdom of our inner being. Christ is only
glorified when He is the undisputed Master of
the heart.

CHAPTER XIV

*" Have I been so long time with you, and yet
hast thou not known Me ? " (v. 9).*

Acquaintance with Christ apart from real
heart knowledge of Him is little short of a
tragedy. Nothing breeds self-sufficiency like
superficial acquaintance with any great truth ;
and in our relation with Christ, Who is the
Truth incarnate, there is a sort of knowledge
which " puffeth up " only to destroy. On the
other hand, there is a knowledge which is life

eternal, toward our personal realization of which all the ministry of God's love is directed.

How fatally easy it is to mistake mere knowledge about Christ for that intimate close relationship which He describes as truly *knowing* Him. For to know Him as Saviour is to experience deliverance from the practice and power of sin. Where such daily victory is not enjoyed, it is obvious that He is not known. To know Him as Friend is to have a sanctifying companionship which lifts the ordinary things of life into the sphere of His pleasure. But where there is little or no love expressed in the deference of choices and pursuits to His desires, it is clear that He is unknown in this relationship. Further, to know Him as Lord, means an implicit obedience to all that is understood as His will. Where, however, there is no doing of the things that He says, no engagement with the enterprises of His Kingdom, no manifested sympathy with His aims, it may be safely concluded that He is not really known.

Unwillingness on the part of any to face the consequence of a revised life such as the knowledge of Christ involves, makes impossible all His further ministry. Satisfied ignorance for ever puts an end to opportunity, and seals the destiny of any man whose self-complacency rules him completely out of the Kingdom.

CHAPTER XV

" He shall testify of Me : and ye also shall bear witness " (*v.* 26).

THE Holy Spirit testifies to Christ's followers of His reality. It is their mission in turn to transmit this testimony to the world. The ultimate objective of the work of the Spirit is the making of Christ known to " the uttermost parts of the earth," through the faithful witness of His disciples. They are to be themselves continually receiving the teaching of the Holy Spirit concerning the Saviour, and are to be as constantly proclaiming Him by life and lip. Their inner life and outward activity are thus to harmonize and to keep pace. The success of their service is directly proportioned to the reality of their sanctity. Their preparation, both of heart and message, is the work of the Comforter. But the responsibility, both of attention and obedience, is their own.

In these days, no less than in those immediately following His own, the great need of His people is that of witnessing power. Although its hostility now assumes more cultured and refined forms than of old, the world is actually as much opposed toward Christ as it ever was. On this account the need of clear and undaunted testimony to His grace and power cannot be overestimated. If the Church does not conquer the world by her witness, it is certain that the world will conquer the Church by her seductions. And it is for this supreme work of bearing witness to Christ that the great promises concerning the Comforter were originally given, and are still available.

The pre-requisite qualification for bearing effective witness is personal knowledge gained by experience, such experience as that into which the Holy Spirit daily brings the willing soul. Heart-attention to His insistent testimony concerning Christ is the open secret of strength for service.

CHAPTER XVI

"When He is come" (*v.* 8).

MISCONCEPTION as to the significance of His title is to a large extent responsible for obscuring the real issues of the work of the Spirit. For the " Comforter " does not merely denote the One Who ministers sympathy, but the One also Who imparts strength. He it is Who not only brings pity in sorrow but power in service. The objective of His ministry is the convincing of the world with regard to the sufficiency of the Saviour, and its conviction with regard to its attitude toward Him. His atonement and all that that mysterious transaction comprehends, His advocacy and all that His presence at the Throne means, His advent and all that His glorious appearing promises—these are the themes upon which the Holy Spirit bases His testimony.

It must be noted that this His mission is accomplished through the Church, both in her corporate life and her individual membership. The testimony of changed lives, the witness of transformed tempers, the proof afforded by renewed desires and recovered powers, is incontrovertible. It is by actually seeing what Christ has done that men are convinced of His claims. Hence there is nothing more important than that those who profess His name should assure themselves as to the character of their relationship to His Spirit. For to be controlled, strengthened, and guided by the Holy Ghost is to be endued with effective power for setting forth Christ convincingly. A faithful witness without the camp always necessitates a faithful worship within the veil. There where the active ministries of the Spirit are renewed to the sincere soul, the quality of service in the world is determined. Remember the work is not ours but His. At the same time is not His only but ours also.

CHAPTER XVII

" *They are not of the world . . . I have sent them into the world* " (*vv.* 16, 18).

NOTHING is clearer than Christ's ideal for His people in respect of their relationship to the world, and all for which it stands. Entire separation in spirit and aim from all that is

"not of the Father," is His determination for
the lives of all who bear His name. Of Himself
He could say in this same High-Priestly prayer—
the most intimate of all the records of His life
—" I am not of the world." And in this, as in all
other realms of life, He is the only safe example
for His people. His separation from the world
was not that of the ascetic who fears the effect
of its contact upon his own purity ; still less was
it that of the superior person who scorns its life
and despises its doings. He was entirely
separated unto the fulfilment of the Father's will,
and in consequence from everything which con-
flicted with this purpose. To Him nothing
mattered beyond the good pleasure of Him that
sent Him. Thus it is that Christ's own life is the
abiding pattern of heart-separation, both from
the alluring and the opposing world. It is by
reason of this same spirit of devotion to the
will of God that His followers are "not of the
world."

As with Himself also, such separation only
precedes and prepares for contact. It is within
this paradox that the true Christian life lies.
For those out of whose heart the world has been
taken are the very ones through whom God
touches the world to save and to heal. They do
not rush to take part in its life at their own
will, but at His appointment. Every necessary
correspondence with its interests is purposely
designed for the showing forth of His glory.

And it is when this devotion to the supreme
characterizes our life, that we are liberated from
the tyranny of mere secondary things. We are
safe only when we seek the sanctification of an
absorbing passion for the will of God.

CHAPTER XVIII

" The cup which my Father hath given me "
(*v.* 11).

BUT a few hours previously Christ had Himself
given a cup to His disciples, in the drinking of
which they should for all time commemorate His
dying love. In the light of this experience, they
were the better able to grasp the import of these
His words, which interpret all that has hitherto
been inexplicable in Him. For His whole life of
temptation and toil is as a cup which has been
put into His hand by the Father. Hence His
willingness to drain it to the dregs. His heroism
is entirely explicable in the light of the love
which He bore, and by which also He was
sustained. He knew nothing of second causes,
and in consequence staggered not at any
experience however seemingly untoward. The
last bitter draining of the cup is not to Him as
defeat in an unequal contest with the world, but
as glorious triumph of love and loyalty. Thus,
in devotion to the Father, He " tasted death for
every man." And His cup of death has in an

inexplicable way opened for us the fountain of life.

In their wider application to the lives of His disciples, these His words define that attitude of submission and trust which conditions a life of peace and power. Those who seek to live in fellowship with Him are still asked : " Can ye drink of the cup that I drink ? "—not that of suffering merely, but of life measured and mixed by the will of God. Only as we accept and drink it, do we find that accession of power for service and sacrifice which makes possible the blessing of other lives through ours. For this is the cup whose draught unfailingly stimulates. It is always possible, however, to turn from love's cup in favour of the world's soothing or intoxicating wines, though to do so is to unwittingly drink to our own destruction.

CHAPTER XIX

" *What I have written I have written* " (*v.* 22).

PILATE'S retort to the dissatisfied Jews may possibly have been a confession of his own inoperative faith ; for in his heart he was convinced of the reality of Christ's claims. If this be so it is the record of his life's greatest tragedy. In any case, however, it is an unconscious expression on his part of vital truth concerning the life of every man. For life is like the writing of a record in which one indelibly sets

down what he is; and each man is one day to
be judged by his own self-written history.

One of life's most profound facts is the permanence of character. What a man writes he
is unable to revise or to erase. No effort of
memory, no act of remorse, no determination to
write better in the future, avails when any one
of us writes the untrue, the unclean, or the
unworthy. Rather, on the contrary, each writer
is faced by the hopeless tyranny of his own
record. What he has written he will in the
nature of the case continue to write. Actions
are immortal things and character is undying.

Part of the Gospel, to those who have written
what is eternally against them, is that Christ
has robbed the past of its despotism. He has
nailed to His Cross all the handwriting of human
guilt and shame; and is able in every life so
to blot it out as to give the opportunity of
writing afresh on a clean page. Then, as with
guided hand the new record is written, this law
of permanence still remains. What we write
under the influence of His Spirit is abiding.
Each of us writes a book of character dedicated
to his Lord; and at the same time adds something also to the record of those other lives which
his life consciously or unconsciously influences.
How carefully, then, should our words and
sentences be formed !

CHAPTER XX

" Then came Jesus, the doors being shut "
(*vv.* 19, 26).

As His disciples on the evening of the Resurrection unwittingly shut the Lord out from their company, so are many lives closed to Him. And, as also on that day, so in this it is the joy of the Saviour to break in upon those who unintentionally have excluded Him from their lives, and who are unspeakably in need of Him. The doors of men's hearts may be closed by engrossment in pleasure or business or friendship, by selfishness of joy or sorrow, by fear of the consequences of identification with Him, or by sin which conscience has already judged. And yet, despite these things, it is really impossible to avoid Christ; for He forces Himself again and again upon our attention. He comes despite closed doors, and reveals Himself in any or all of His guises as Friend, Succourer, Redeemer, King. For He sees and interprets our imperfectly understood longings, and puts the best possible construction upon the activities by which we seek to realize our ideals. By the written Word or the spoken message, by uncontrolled memory or inexplicable impulse, in the glory of the noontide or in the quiet watches of the night, He is ever coming to us through our shut doors, offering Himself and all that He is and has for our salvation and life.

His coming thus is ever with the same intent as was His appearance in the Upper Room. His first word is always one of benediction, " Peace be unto you " ; while He shows the wounded hands and feet which declare that the free gift He bestows has been dearly purchased. In that sanctifying consciousness, He sends His people forth into the world, as light-bearers in the darkness, and as ambassadors at the court of His enemy : " As My Father hath sent Me, so send I you."

It is the dawning hope and the crowning glory also of any life to open wide its hitherto closed doors that " the King of Glory may come in." For He comes to make us sons of God.

CHAPTER XXI

" Lord, what shall this man do ? " (*v.* 21).

T<small>HE</small> danger of theorizing even in the supreme crises of life is never far from any one of us. We are always prone to receive and pass on the message of Christ to other lives, instead of first applying its force to ourselves. Real interest and concern in the souls of others is truly an evidence of Christ-compassion. But it may be also a mere curiosity, whose effect is but to deprive and deteriorate our own relationship with Him.

Thus it was with Peter, even in the most

solemn and tender experience which his contact
with Christ had afforded. Restored to fellowship which sin had forfeited, rekindled to love
which floods of anguish had wellnigh drowned,
and recommissioned to the service from which
he was self-excluded, he was even yet unable
to concentrate upon the Saviour and upon his
own soul. His mind was partly upon the
fellow-disciple; and he unwittingly attempted to
divert the intensely personal statement of
Christ's interest over a wider and more general
area. And in this he is not alone. For to
many an one the river of life has become a mere
marsh. They turn the Divine message into
a mere theory, and thus lose its peculiarly
personal message of life. Christ has a message
for John also; but for the moment His concern
is with Peter!

The first law of the new life is to follow Him,
even though we do so solitarily. Nor can we
ever fail thus to influence our fellows, as we
courageously set ourselves to tread the pathway
of discipleship whose end is so frankly disclosed
by our Lord. But they in turn must follow
Him and not us. Our concern for them must
at all times be utterly disinterested, and
prompted only by desire for His unquestioned
glory. And our obedience must be altogether
uninfluenced by anything of another's life. This
indeed is the sum total of the Gospel demand.